UNDERSTANDING CHRISTIANITY – SALVATION

BY

FRANK B. HOLE

First published 1998

ISBN 0 901860 17 4

Published by Scripture Truth Publications
Coopies Way, Coopies Lane, Morpeth, Northumberland, NE61 6JN
Scripture Truth is an imprint of Central Bible Hammond Trust,
a charitable trust.

Typesetting and cover design by Create Publishing, Bath.
Printed in the UK by Bookcraft, Bath.

FOREWORD

F. B. Hole was a student, and an able expositor, of Scripture. He was for many years the editor of the magazine, *Scripture Truth*. His writings, always clear and direct, have helped many in their understanding of Scripture and the One whom Scripture sets forth, our Lord Jesus Christ.

Some of these writings are reissued in this volume and its companion, *Understanding Christianity – Key Teachings*, in order that they may be available to, and of blessing to, the wider Christian public. They are reissued so that the clear teaching of Scripture might be set forth in a day when so many of the basic tenets of the Christian faith are under attack.

Dr. G. Hughes, Liverpoool, 1998

PREFACE

The contents of this volume originally appeared under two titles, *The Great Salvation* and *Outlines of Truth*. The original preface to *The Great Salvation* appears below:

"The Scriptures themselves speak of the "great salvation", which has reached us through the Gospel. We, who have experienced the saving grace of God, know something of its greatness, but it is only as we search the Scriptures and investigate its details that the magnitude of what God has brought to pass begins to dawn upon us.

In these pages the main details are taken up one by one. If all be put together, the great salvation of God is before us; and it is important to remember that each is but one part of a great whole. They are considered separately in order that we may gain a fuller understanding of each part, and thereby more fully understand the whole.

We can no more apprehend the whole Divine plan at one moment than we can see all four sides of a building from one viewpoint. We have to content ourselves with one thing at a time. If this book helps any Christians to a deeper appreciation of the wonders wrought of God through the Gospel, not only will they be spiritually helped but God will be glorified."

F. B. Hole

CONTENTS

Chapter One

———————

FORGIVENESS

When the first stirrings of the Spirit of God took place within us, the effect in almost every case was that we became conscious of our sins and of the guilt that attached to them, and consequently we became seekers after forgiveness. We wanted to be forgiven, and to know it.

The reader has, we trust, the knowledge of forgiveness, yet it may be well if we begin by surveying the teaching of Scripture on this subject, and thus aim at obtaining an orderly understanding of this great, fundamental blessing of the Gospel.

First of all then, let us observe that when sin entered into the world by the transgression of Adam, and the human race consequently lapsed into an utterly fallen and sinful condition, its effects were manifold and went far beyond the incurring of guilt. Yet the first and most obvious effect was that Adam became a guilty and conscious-stricken man. As men multiplied it had to be said that, "all the world" was "guilty before God" (Rom. 3:19), and this means, since guilt is an intensely individual matter, that every individual composing the world, every one of us is guilty.

But the Scripture speaks of, "them that are contentious, and do not obey the truth" (Rom. 2:8). Many such are to be found, who are by no means disposed to acknowledge their guilt, but rather challenge the foundations on which rests the very idea of being guilty before God. They assert on the contrary the innate goodness of all men, who are, so they say, always struggling upwards. Some of these contentious folk go so far as to deny all fixed standards of right and wrong. Good and evil are words of only relative force, since to them "good" is that which is approved by the most enlightened sections of humanity in any given age, and "evil" is that which their mind repudiates. It therefore follows that "right" and "wrong" are values which fluctuate according to the fashions of the age in matters of morality. The human mind is left the whole arbiter of such questions, and consequently the only guilt they know is that which may be incurred before men as the result of flouting the standards erected by the most enlightened and advanced amongst them. The utmost verdict that they can approve of is therefore, *guilty before men.*

The epistle to the Romans, on the other hand, begins with *God*, and we do not have to travel far into its contents before we arrive at the verdict against us of, *"guilty before God."*

In its opening chapter we read of,

"The Gospel of God"
"The Son of God"
"The power of God"
"The righteousness of God"
"The wrath of God"
"The glory of God"
"The judgment of God"

and God, whose power and righteousness and wrath and glory and judgment are revealed, is "the Creator" (1:25). At once therefore we leave the quagmire of human standards and opinions for the sure rock of divine truth, and we find ourselves standing in the presence of the Creator, who is marked by fixed and unalterable righteousness.

Much may be needed indeed before the conviction of guilt is driven home effectively into the consciousness of the individual sinner. This may not be so difficult a matter with peoples who have lapsed into the barbarism that so frequently accompanies heathenism. Such are in view in Romans 1:18–32, and they stand without excuse, and consequently their mouths are shut. The mere recital of the enormous evils into which they had fallen, as a result of turning away from the knowledge of God, is sufficient. In their case no reasoning is necessary in order to convict and silence.

But at different times in the world's history, nations, though pagan, have evolved amongst themselves systems of natural culture and civilization. Such were the ancient Greeks, and to these, Romans 2:1–16 is addressed. In their case the dark cesspool of iniquity was partly covered up by fine systems of philosophical thought and ethical teaching. They condemned the poor, unlettered barbarian yet they themselves did the same things in a more refined way. They too are pronounced to be "inexcusable," yet some very pointed reasoning, coupled with sharp home-thrusts of the keen blade of truth, is necessary before the conviction of it can be driven home. In the course of reasoning they are reminded that, "The judgment of God is according to truth"; that the day is coming for the revelation of "the righteous judgment of God"; and that "there is no respect of persons with God".

By the combination of these three facts their escape from the judgment of God is rendered impossible. If His judgment were sometimes according to mere outward appearances, or if it occasionally lapsed from strict righteousness or deviated because of favouritism or other personal considerations, then there might be some chance of escape. It is however *"according to truth,"* and hence the exact reality of things will be dragged into the light of day. It is *"righteous,"* and hence absolute and inflexible justice will prevail. There is *"no respect of persons,"* hence nothing will turn God from a judgment of absolute righteousness in the light of absolute truth. This must shut the mouth of the most civilized and the most cultured, and convict them too as "guilty before God."

Lastly there were the Jews, a people brought under a culture which was not merely natural but divine. Romans 2:17–3:20 is addressed to such, and in this passage we have not merely reasoning but the decisive evidence of their own Scriptures. Their indictment is couched in terms culled from their own law, and at the close the weight of this Scriptural evidence is driven home into their consciences by the fact that "what things soever the law saith, *it saith to them who are under the law"*; that is, to the Jews. The sweeping accusations and condemnation of the law was aimed therefore, not at the barbarian nor the Greek, but at the opinionated and self-righteous Jew, that even his mouth might be stopped, and thus all the world become "guilty before God."

Guilt being established, forgiveness becomes an urgent necessity. Hence we find it placed in the very forefront of the instructions given by the risen Lord to His disciples. In Luke 24:45–48 He told the eleven that "remission of sins should be preached in His name among all nations." In Acts 26:16–18 we have the apostle Paul's account of how in a heavenly vision he heard the voice of the Glorified One, sending him to the Gentiles, "to open their eyes . . . that they may receive forgiveness of sins." How these commissions were carried out the Acts bears witness. To the multitude in Jerusalem, who on the day of Pentecost were pricked in their heart, Peter spoke of "the remission of sins" (2:38). Before the council he again testified of "forgiveness of sins" (5:31). Again to the Gentile Cornelius and his friends he proclaimed that "through His name whosoever believeth in Him shall receive remission of sins" (10:43). To the mixed crowd in the synagogue at Antioch Paul declared, "Be it known . . . that through this Man is preached unto you the forgiveness of sins" (13:38).

In each case, of the six quoted above, the same Greek word occurs in the original, though translated both as remission and forgiveness in the Authorized Version. It signifies simply "a sending away" or "a release" and this is just what a guilty sinner needs as regards his sins. Let them be *sent away or dismissed* by the One against whom his guilt has been incurred, and what a happy *release* is his! Now this is just what every child of God is entitled to enjoy. "I write unto you little children" said the aged apostle John, "because your sins are forgiven you [are dismissed and sent away] for His name's sake" (1 John 2:12).

It is in the epistle to the Romans, as we have seen, that the Holy Ghost pronounces the verdict of "guilty before God" against the whole human race. We might naturally have expected therefore that immediately following this we should have found a full unfolding of forgiveness. As a matter of fact however the word for forgiveness only occurs once in the whole epistle, and that when the Apostle cites David's words from Psalm 32. The blessedness of the man to whom God imputes righteousness without works is described by David saying, "Blessed are they whose iniquities are forgiven" (4:6, 7). This shows us however that the imputation of righteousness — *i.e.* justification — is in this passage practically equivalent to forgiveness.

The words that are so much used in the early chapters of Romans are *righteousness and justification*, and they are on the whole words of great fulness. One cannot have one's sins forgiven without being justi-

fied, nor *vice versa*; yet in the main the force of forgiveness is negative —
we lose our sins: the main force of justification is positive — we gain
righteousness.

It has been asserted that everybody is forgiven. Is
there any sense in which such a statement is true?

No. It is of course a wonderful fact that, "God was in Christ, reconciling the world unto Himself, not imputing their trespasses unto
them" (2 Cor. 5:19). Hence the Lord's words to the sinful woman,
"Neither do I condemn thee" (John 8:11). God's overtures of mercy, in
Christ present upon earth, were however rejected. It is also a wonderful
fact that, His overtures being rejected, He has taken advantage of the
death and resurrection of Christ to send out a world-wide message of
forgiveness, so that in the Gospel today forgiveness is preached to all,
and He is presented as a forgiving God. (See Luke 24:46,47).

Instead of the rejection of Christ being followed by a declaration
of war, and the hurling of Heaven's thunderbolts against a rebellious
world, God has, as it were, established a lengthy armistice, during which
time an amnesty for all rebels is being proclaimed. If any rebel humbles
himself and turns to the Saviour in faith, *he is forgiven*. It is true therefore
that *there is forgiveness for everybody*; but in no sense is it true that
everybody is forgiven.

In His parable of the two debtors in Luke 7, the
Lord did teach however that both were forgiven by
the creditor. Was not Simon, the self-righteous
Pharisee, as much forgiven therefore as the
repentant sinner?

"He frankly forgave them *both*." Both therefore *were* frankly
forgiven. The two words "frankly forgave" are the translation of one
Greek word — not the usual word for forgiveness but a word meaning,
"to show grace to". The Lord Jesus therefore in His parable represented
God as acting in a forgiving spirit and showing grace towards men, no
matter what the depth of their sin. This is exactly God's attitude today.

Later in the story the Lord did utter the usual word for forgiveness. He said of the woman, "her sins, which are many, are forgiven." To her He said, "Thy sins are forgiven." *Her* sins, then, were definitely dismissed, for she believed in the Saviour and came to Him.

Grace was indeed shown even to proud Simon, and he was not brought instantly and summarily into judgment for his sins. In that sense he was "frankly forgiven", but the Lord never told him that his sins had been definitely dismissed. Only the repentant sinner is thus forgiven, in the ordinary meaning of the word.

Is it a fact that when a sinner repents and believes he receives forgiveness once and for all?

Certainly it is. In the argument on the subject of sacrifice, contained in Hebrews 9:1–10:18, the fact is one of the main points. In that great passage it is affirmed no less than six times that the sacrifice of Christ was *one* and offered *once*. It is also asserted that those who approach God as worshippers on the ground of His sacrifice are purged *once*, and consequently draw near with perfected consciences (10:1, 2). The perfection of which the first verse speaks is "pertaining to the conscience" (9:9), and founded upon the *one* perfect cleansing, or purging, that has reached them. We stand before God in an eternal forgiveness.

To this it is objected by some, that if a believer is taught that at his conversion he obtained complete forgiveness, it is sure to provoke him to carelessness and license. Might it not be better to say that all is forgiven up to the point of conversion?

No one would object in this way but those who deny, or at least overlook, the fact that we are not converted without being born again and thereby becoming possessed of a nature that hates evil. Once give this fact its due weight and the whole case wears a different aspect. Further, not only are we born again and forgiven but we receive the Holy Spirit of God to dwell in us, and we come under the teaching of grace, of which Titus 2:11–14, speaks.

We must remember that though forgiveness is ministered to us when we believe, yet it was procured for us by the sacrifice of Christ; and *all* our sins — not only those up to the point of conversion — were future, when He died and rose again.

We must remember also that God, as Father, does deal with us, His children, as and when we sin. Upon confession we are forgiven and cleansed, for "we have an Advocate with the Father, Jesus Christ the righteous" (1 John 1:9–2:1). But this is the Father's forgiveness, restoring us to communion, and not the eternal forgiveness, which we receive at the outset from Him as Judge of all.

What then is meant by, "the remission of sins that are past", which we read of in Romans 3:25?

All depends upon what is the fixed point, in relation to which the sins are past. If we also read verse 26, it will be apparent that the contrast is between what God did as to sins in the past time and what He does "at this time"; the great event dividing the two times being the first advent of Christ. It is evident therefore that in speaking of "sins that are past" the apostle Paul referred to the sins of the believers who lived in the past dispensation. His words had no reference to certain sins of a believer being past, if viewed from the standpoint of his conversion.

The sins of these pre-Christian era believers were remitted by God. "Remission" here is not the ordinary word for forgiveness, but one which means, "a passing by". The meaning of the passage is, that when the propitiatory work of Christ became an accomplished fact, it at once showed forth that God had been righteous in passing by the sins of Old Testament believers, just as it also vindicates His righteousness in this Gospel age in justifying the believer in Jesus.

Chapter Two

JUSTIFICATION

To be justified is to be cleared from every charge that could be brought against us. That this is the meaning is very apparent in the Apostle's words, recorded in Acts 13:39, "By Him all that believe are justified from all things, from which ye could not be justified by the law of Moses." The law could most effectually impeach us. It could lay sins to our charge and bring a righteous condemnation upon us. Only by Christ can the believer be righteously cleared from every charge in the impeachment, so that the sentence of condemnation is lifted off him.

Condemnation then is the state and position from which we pass when we are justified. It is evidently the opposite to justification, just as guilt is the opposite to forgiveness. Yet justification, as set before us in Scripture, implies more than the negative blessing of our being completely and righteously extricated from the condemnation under which we lay: it involves our standing before God in Christ, in a righteousness which is positive and divine.

We must again turn to the Epistle to the Romans. In chapter 3:19 we find that, "all the world" stands convicted as "guilty before God". In verse 20 we find that the law can only convict: there is no justification for us in it. In verse 21, begins the unfolding of God's way of justifying the ungodly.

Inasmuch as "all have sinned, and come short of the glory of God", it is not surprising that God should bring into manifestation His righteousness. Man having manifested his sin in all its blackness, it was to be expected that, by way of contrast, God would manifest His righteousness in all its brightness; condemning the sinner, and thus clearing

Himself of the smallest suspicion that He in any way condoned the sin. What is so wonderful is that now God's righteousness has been manifested in such a way as to be "*unto*" or "*towards* all, and upon all them that believe". Righteousness, God's righteousness, is, as it were, stretching out its hands benignly towards all men instead of frowning upon them; and as for those that believe, it descends upon them as a robe, so that in the presence of God they stand invested in it. And all this is done without righteousness in any way losing its own proper character, or ceasing to be what it is.

Upon first hearing this, our impulse might be to exclaim, "Impossible! Such a thing as this is absolutely impossible!" We might be disposed to reason that, while mercy might act in this fashion, but at the expense of righteousness, righteousness itself could never do so.

Yet righteousness does so act, since it has now been manifested in Christ, who has been set forth by God as a "propitiation", or "mercy-seat" (verse 25). When upon the cross His blood was shed, there was fulfilled the Antitype of the blood-sprinkled mercy-seat of Tabernacle days. Redemption was wrought "in Christ Jesus", (verse 24), and the greatest display of divine righteousness, which the universe will ever witness, took place. By and by the righteousness of God will be manifested in the judgment and everlasting overthrow of the ungodly. That solemn hour will witness no mean display of divine righteousness, yet not so profound and wonderful as in that yet more solemn hour when God judged and put to grief His own spotless Son for us. The cross of Christ will remain to all eternity the greatest manifestation of the righteousness of God. It manifested equally His love of course, as Romans 5:8 declares, but had it not manifested His righteousness it could not have manifested His love.

The death of Christ has displayed the righteousness of God in a twofold way. First, as regards His dealings as to the sins of believers in the past dispensation (verse 25); and second, as to the sins of believers in this present age (verse 26). Before Christ came God passed over the sins of His people, though as yet no perfect satisfaction for them had been made to Him. In this present time He is justifying the believer in Jesus. Have all these dealings on God's part been conducted in strict righteousness? They have, and the death of Christ declares it; showing that when

God passed over sins during the bygone dispensation He was absolutely justified in doing so, as also He is just in justifying the believer today.

The death of Christ was primarily the offering of Himself *to God* as a sacrifice of infinite value and fragrance. Propitiation was thereby effected, and satisfaction made, so that the claims of divine righteousness have been met and vindicated in regard to the whole matter of man's sin.

Secondarily, however, His offering was *for us,* *i.e.* for all true believers. Such are entitled to view the Saviour as their Substitute, and to translate Romans 4:25 out of the plural into the singular, and say, He "was delivered for *my* offences, and was raised again for *my* justification." He was delivered to death and judgment with our sins in view: He was raised again from the dead with our justification in view.

Many there are who in this matter cut the Gospel in half, and ignore the second part of it to their own great loss. Full assurance cannot be enjoyed if the meaning of Christ's resurrection be overlooked. The bearing of our sins and their penalty was indeed accomplished in His death, but the declaration and proof of our clearance is in His resurrection. Without this second part settled peace cannot be known.

To illustrate the point, let us suppose a man condemned to six months' imprisonment for an offence, and another as a substitute permitted to take his place. When the prison gates swing to, shutting the substitute within and leaving the offender in liberty without, the latter might well exclaim of his friend, "He has been delivered to prison for my offence," but further than that he cannot go for the moment. It would be premature for him to add, "and consequently it is impossible that I should ever see the inside of that prison, as the penalty for what I have done."

What if his good friend breathed his last at the end of two months, leaving four months of the sentence unexpired? The Authorities would righteously lay their hands on the original offender and demand that he himself should work out the remainder of his term.

But, on the other hand, if a week or so before the six months were up he should suddenly come upon his kindly substitute walking in the street, and on expressing his surprise, learn that, having by good behaviour earned a small remission of the sentence, he was really discharged as a free man, he would instantly be able to say, "Why, you are released from prison for my justification!" He would argue in his own mind, *and rightly*, "If he is discharged from prison as free from all further liability, completely cleared in regard to my offence, then *I am discharged, I am free, I am cleared!*"

Viewed in this light, the resurrection of Christ is seen to be the Divine declaration of the complete clearance of the one who believes in Him. It is, we need hardly say, much else besides.

Having said this much, we must now observe that God Himself is not only the Source of our justification but He who justifies us. "It is God that justifieth" (Rom. 8:33). From His lips came the sentence against us as sinners. Equally from His lips comes forth the declaration of our clearance as believers in Jesus. Our justification therefore is complete and authoritative. No one can condemn us.

But on our side faith is necessary; for only believers are justified. In this sense we are, "justified by faith" (Rom. 5:1). Only as yielding "the obedience of faith" to our Lord Jesus do we come in under the benefits of His work. He is "the Author of eternal salvation" *only* to "all them that obey Him" (Heb. 5:9). Faith is the link which connects us with Him and the justifying merits of His blood.

One further thought as to justification is presented to us in Romans 5:18. In nearly every other passage where justification is mentioned it stands in relation to our sins — "of many offences unto justification," as Romans 5:16 puts it. In verse 18, however, another view of the matter appears, and *sin*, the root, rather than *sins*, the fruit, is in question. The one righteousness of the cross has its bearing "towards" all "unto justification of life" (J.N.D. trans.).

To understand this phrase, the whole passage — verse 12 to the end of the chapter — must be considered. By nature all men stand related to Adam, as the head and fountain of their race. By grace, and through Christ's death and resurrection, all believers stand related to Him, as the Head and Fountain of that spiritual race to which they now belong. As grafted into Christ, if we may so speak, they participate in His life and nature; and as in the life of Christ they are cleared judicially from all the consequences that formerly lay on them as in the life of Adam. A very wonderful thing, this, and one that is too often overlooked by us all.

Justification then, as the Epistle to the Romans presents it, not only means a complete clearance from all offences and the condemnation attaching to our fallen Adamic nature, inasmuch as now, by God's act, we stand in Christ risen from the dead. Blessed be God, for such a clearance as this!

> You have not alluded to the righteousness of Christ being imputed to us? Why?

Because that idea is not found in Scripture. There is no difficulty in finding there the righteousness of Christ. That was absolutely perfect, and hence, being without blemish, He was qualified to be the "Lamb" of sacrifice on our behalf. But we are justified by His blood and not by His perfect life. He died for us, but in no place is it said that He kept the law for us. Had He done so we should after all be standing in a merely *legal* righteousness before God; and by that we mean, a righteousness which merely goes to the length of keeping the law of Moses. Our righteousness before God would after all be just that righteousness of the law, of which Moses speaks (see Rom. 10:5); though worked out, not by ourselves, but by Christ on our behalf.

> But surely righteousness is imputed, for we read in Romans 4 that, "God imputeth righteousness without works", and again that, "it was imputed to him for righteousness". What then do these expressions mean?

If that chapter be carefully read it will be noticed that the words, *counted, imputed, reckoned,* occur several times. All three words have the same force, being translations of the same word, which is most nearly expressed by the word *reckoned.* "Abraham believed God and it was counted unto him for righteousness." That is, Abraham *was reckoned righteous* or *held to be righteous* by God, in virtue of his faith. The little word "for" is apt to mislead, as it may suggest the idea of faith being a kind of substitute for righteousness, something which may be "transmuted into righteousness", more nearly gives the sense. If you have a *New Translation* (J.N. Darby) with full notes, turn up this verse and consult the footnote as to the translation, which is very illuminating.

The argument of Romans 4, then, is that whether it be Abraham of old, or believers in Christ today, there is only one way by which we may be reckoned righteous before God, the great Judge of all; and that is, by faith without works. *Without works*, mark you! Not even the perfect works of Christ, everyone of them done in righteousness, come in here: another proof, if it were needed, that we are not made righteous by a certain quantity of His law-keeping being imputed to us. What does come in is His death and resurrection. This underlies the whole of the chapter, and is plainly expressed at the end. Read verse 25 and see.

That verse has been taken to mean that just as Jesus died because we were sinners, so He was raised again because we had been justified in His death. Is this a correct view of it?

You have but to read on into chapter 5 to find that it is not correct. Our chapter divisions are sometimes not natural but artificial, breaking into the middle of a paragraph. This is a case in point. He "was raised again for our justification. Therefore being justified by faith, we have peace with God."

The interpretation you mention presents our justification as an accomplished fact when Jesus died, and His resurrection to be the consequence of it. But this entirely elminates our faith from the question; and our faith cannot be eliminated thus, in view of the first verse of chapter 5. His death was in view of our sins, and is *the basis of our justification*; but that is another matter.

His resurrection was, in the first place, the declaration of the blessed fact, that He who stooped under the weight of God's judgment against sin, is for ever clear of it. In the second place, it was in view of the clearance of all who believe in Him.

This we have just been enforcing and illustrating. He was delivered to death with our sins in view: He was raised again with our justification in view. But the justification of each individual only becomes effective as and when they *believe*.

Chapter Three

———————

REDEMPTION

Not only has sin plunged us into guilt, and brought us face to face with condemnation, but it has entangled us in bondage from which we are utterly unable to extricate ourselves.

Then, as regards the Gospel, not only does it proclaim forgiveness in relation to our guilt, and justification instead of condemnation, but it reveals to us God, acting as a Redeemer, delivering His people from bondage, and thereby freeing His inheritance from all the encumbrances under which formerly it lay.

There is a good deal about redemption in the Old Testament, and one of the words used for it has the meaning, it is said, of, "freeing, whether by avenging or repaying."

In Exodus we find the great *type* of redemption. To the children of Israel, who were just down-trodden slaves, Jehovah said, "I will redeem you with a stretched-out arm, and with great judgments" (6:6). So this was clearly a case of redemption by *avenging* their wrongs upon Egypt; though we also see the *repayment* of what they owed to God as sinners in the shed blood of the lamb. When all was effectively accomplished we find Israel on the further banks of the Red Sea, singing, "Thou in Thy mercy hast led forth Thy people which Thou hast redeemed" (15:13).

A striking *illustration* of redemption is given to us in the book of Ruth. Boaz redeemed Elimelech's inheritance by payment, and this involved the raising up of the name of the dead by the taking of Ruth. Boaz took both to himself — the wife and the inheritance — by right of redemption.

Both in the type and in the illustration bondage of one sort or another was in question. In the type, Israel were in sore bondage under Pharaoh, and again and again in reference to them Egypt is called, "the house of bondage". In the illustration, the inheritance of the dead Elimelech was in danger of passing into other hands, and the widow and daughter-in-law of lapsing into a condition of servitude. This disaster was averted by the action of Boaz as their kinsman-redeemer.

Turning to the New Testament, we find that redemption as well as justification is mentioned in Romans 3. We are said to be, "justified . . . through the redemption that is in Christ Jesus". This serves to emphasize an important point; namely, that these different aspects of the work of Christ and its effects are most intimately connected, so that we cannot have one without the other. Yet, though never to be divided the one from the other, they are clearly to be distinguished. The earlier part of Romans 3 has brought before us not only the guilt and condemnation of sin, but also its bondage. The word itself is not actually used until chapter 8 is reached, yet the idea is there, for the Apostle says, "We have before proved both Jews and Gentiles, that they are all under sin." To be "under sin" is to be under the power of it, that is, to be in bondage to it. Christ has done the great work which avails to pay off all the liabilities under which we lay, and thus redemption is in Him for us.

If we read on through the Epistle to the Romans, we discover, in chapters 6, 7 and the early part of 8, how we are actually set free from the tyranny of sin and the yoke of the law; all of which had proved us to be in "the bondage of corruption". This phrase is actually used in chapter 8:21, where we learn that the whole earthly creation lies under its thrall, but that all shall be delivered and brought into "the liberty of the glory of the children of God". When the Lord comes and the children of God stand forth in their glory, then there will be proclaimed a jubilee of liberty for all creation.

For that moment we wait, and in verse 23 it is said that for us it will be, "the adoption, to wit, the redemption of our body". Here again redemption appears, since the point in question is deliverance from bondage; and the redemption of our bodies is presented to us as a freedom gained by avenging, as it says, "I will redeem them from death: O death, I will be thy plagues; O grave, I will be thy destruction" (Hosea

13:14). This scripture is alluded to and applied to the resurrection of the body in 1 Corinthians 15:55. In that glad day the bodies of all God's saints will be delivered from the grip of death, the last enemy.

The redemption work of Christ also comes rather prominently before us in the Epistle to the Galatians. We read that, "Christ hath redeemed us from the curse of the law" (3:13), and this was by paying the price on our behalf, for it adds, "being made a curse for us."

But not only did we lie under the curse of the law but the law itself held us in bondage. We were "in bondage under the elements of the world" (4:3). Lower down in the chapter, Paul speaks of, "the weak and beggarly elements, whereunto ye desire again to be in bondage" (4:9). The word translated "elements" has the force of "principles", and is so translated in Hebrews 5:12. We may at first be inclined to wonder that such terms as these — almost contemptuous terms — should be applied to the law, which was given of God, but the "we" of chapter 4:3, clearly indicates Jews, just as the "ye" of verse 6 indicates the Galatian Gentiles. Both were under bondage to the principles of the world. The law of Moses made no difference as to this. It brought in the demands of God, but they were to be met according to the principles of the world. The root principle of the law was that the favour which men were to receive from God was to be wholly determined by what they rendered to Him in obedience. This is altogether a principle of the world, whereas grace is not. There was no bringing in of principles which lie outside the world altogether, as is the case in Christianity.

From the principles of the world, whether found in Judaism or elsewhere, weak and beggarly as they are, Christ has redeemed us that we might receive the adoption of sons. Such is the mighty grace of God.

Redemption, as we have seen, extends even to the resurrection of the body, and this side of the matter we again find in the Epistle to the Ephesians. While we read of, "redemption through His blood, the forgiveness of sins" (1:7), we also read of the earnest of the Spirit being, "until the redemption of the purchased possession" (1:14), and of our being, "sealed unto the day of redemption" (4:30). The first of these passages speaks of that which is ours today, and which never will be more ours than it is today. The second and third speak of redemption in a form for which we wait. *All* that Christ has bought by His death shall be taken from beneath the sway of the usurper and of every adverse power. As far as our bodies are concerned the moment will arrive at the coming of the Lord Jesus for His saints. That having taken place, the Lord will set His hand to the work of redeeming by power from the hand of the enemy all the rest of the possession which He purchased by His blood.

This coming redemption by power is a great theme of Old Testament prophecy. It is particularly prominent in the latter part of Isaiah. Israel needed redemption for he was being trodden down by the Gentiles and hence is addressed as "thou worm Jacob"; and Jehovah announces Himself as, "thy Redeemer, the Holy One of Israel" (41:14). Having introduced Himself in this light, He continues to speak of Himself as Redeemer until chapter 63 is reached, where the prophet sees Him in vision, coming forth from Edom and Bozrah, because at last, as He says, "The day of vengeance is in Mine heart, and the year of My redeemed is come." The redemption of the true Israel of God means vengeance upon all their foes.

Yet in the midst of these striking chapters with their many promises of a coming redemption by means of the avenging might of God, we get a most marvellous prediction concerning the yet deeper matter of redemption by means of the death of Christ. We read, "Ye have sold yourselves for nought; and ye shall be redeemed without money" (52:3). This is followed by the heart-moving chapter wherein the blessed Servant of Jehovah is portrayed as the suffering, dying One, whose soul is made an offering for sin by Jehovah Himself. The Redeemer is going to "come to Zion, and to them that turn from transgression in Jacob" (59:20), but this is only possible inasmuch as He has first redeemed them without money as the result of the travail of His soul.

We sometimes hear people speak of "the finished work of redemption". Is it quite correct to speak thus in view of the fact that we still wait for the redemption of our bodies?

It is to this scripture perhaps that Peter referred when he wrote, "Ye were not redeemed with corruptible things, as silver and gold . . . but with the precious blood of Christ, as of a lamb without blemish and without spot" (1 Peter 1:18,19). Isaiah 52 speaks of our being "redeemed without money." Isaiah 53 of the One who "had done no violence, neither was any deceit in His mouth", and yet "He is brought as a lamb to the slaughter" for our redemption.

Not quite correct, no doubt. But when people speak thus they are probably dwelling in their minds exclusively upon the work of redemption by blood. That part of the great work is indeed finished, and never to be repeated. Propitiation has been made once and for all, so when it is a question of that, or of forgiveness, or of justification, there is no future aspect to be considered. But there is a future aspect of redemption, as we have seen. And it is well to remember that, and to speak with care lest we obscure the finishing touches which are to be given to the work of redemption in the days to come.

On the other hand, seeing there is this future aspect of redemption, is it quite right if we speak of ourselves as *having been* redeemed? Ought we not rather to speak of ourselves as being redeemed?

"We have redemption through His blood." So says the Scripture twice over — in Ephesians 1 and Colossians 1. Therefore we cannot be wrong if we say with all boldness that *we have it*. But it is *through His blood*, you notice. Redemption, in that aspect of it, is wholly in the past. The redemption of our bodies is wholly in the future. But redemption is never presented in Scripture as a process which is going on. It is never said that we are being redeemed day by day, though there is such a thing as day-by-day salvation.

Is it not a rather uncomfortable doctrine that redemption, a certain part of it at least, lies in the future? Might there not be a loophole here for just a little uncertainty to creep in?

If redemption were a human work, or if even a small human element entered the question, there would be uncertainty right enough — not just a little creeping in, but floods of it sweeping everything before them. We may well thank God that it is a work not human but Divine. God never leaves His work uncompleted: this we may see in the history of the typical redemption which He wrought in Egypt. He did not redeem the children of Israel by the blood of the Paschal lamb and then forget them, so that they remained under the taskmasters of Egypt. No. All those whom He redeemed by blood He also redeemed by His mighty power clean out of Egypt. Each, down to the youngest child, had to go; not even a hoof was to be left behind. God will complete His work concerning us. Every one redeemed by the precious blood of Christ will be there when at His second coming He redeems the bodies of His saints.

Is redemption the great end that God has in view for His people?

No. It is not the end in view, but rather the all-important means to that end. In the old dispensation the purpose that God had in view was that Israel should be His own peculiar nation, serving Him in the land He had given them. He had to redeem them out of Egypt in order that this might be brought to pass, for they could not serve Him so long as they were in servitude to Pharaoh. In our case the end in view is of a much higher order.

It is His purpose that we should be sons before Him in love. Ephesians 1:5–7 speaks of this; and we find that redemption is necessary as a means to that end. Colossians 1 shows that we are made meet for inheritance of the saints in light; and again redemption is mentioned as necessary for this. Peter, in his first epistle, instructs us that God purposes to have us as a holy priesthood to offer up spiritual sacrifices acceptable to Him by Jesus Christ; but as a preliminary to this he speaks of our having been redeemed by the precious blood of Christ.

Other scriptures to the same effect might be cited. God has many thoughts for us His people, but their fulfilment is only possible upon the basis of redemption. First we must be redeemed from every adverse power. Then God has His way with us to carry out His bright designs.

The book of Ruth shows us that in Israel only certain kinsmen had the right of redemption. Has this any significance for us?

Undoubtedly it has. To purchase was one thing — anyone might do that: to redeem was another. The nearest kinsman had the first right, but one had to be a kinsman to have any right of redemption at all. There is no kinship between angels and men: hence no angel could redeem a man even if he had possessed the power to do so. The Lord Jesus did not become an angel; He became a Man and thereby established that kinship which qualified Him to become our Kinsman–Redeemer. How important then is the true manhood of our Lord.

Hebrews 2 does not contain the word redeem. But it tells us that He did not take hold of angels, but the seed of Abraham, when He undertook through death to annul him that had the power of death and deliver us — that is, to accomplish our redemption.

We read in Ephesians 1:14 of "the redemption of the purchased possession." Should we then draw a distinction between purchase and redemption?

We believe that we should. We might put it in this way — redemption involves purchase, but purchase very often has nothing to do with redemption. Believers are said to be "bought with a price" (1 Cor. 6:20). But false teachers will go so far as "denying the Lord that bought them, and bring upon themselves swift destruction" (2 Peter 2:1). The buying of believers involves their redemption. The buying of the false teachers, who go to destruction, did not involve their redemption; had it done so destruction would not be their end. By His death the Lord Jesus has acquired purchase rights over all things, even where He has not redeemed them.

In Ephesians 1:14 however the point is not exactly this, but rather that what He has purchased by His death He will ultimately redeem by His power from every adverse force. It is really the distinction between redemption by blood and redemption by power.

Chapter Four

———————

RECONCILIATION

A number of different words have been employed by the Spirit of God to convey to us the far-reaching effects of the work of Christ. Reconciliation is one of them, and it possesses great definiteness of meaning. It carries us further into the positive blessing of the Gospel than do justification or redemption. The very idea it expresses belongs to the New Testament.

At first sight this hardly appears to be the case. A good concordance (such as "Young's") shows us that the word occurs nine times in the Old Testament; but on closer inspection we discover that in seven of these it is used to translate the ordinary word for "atonement." In one case it is used for a word that has to do with offering. The remaining occurrence of the word comes nearer to the New Testament meaning (in 1 Samuel 29:4), but there God is not in question.

In the New Testament there are three passages that deal with reconciliation — Romans 5, 2 Corinthians 5, Colossians 1 — and there is also a reference to it in Ephesians 2.

Justification is needed by us because of the guilt of sin and the condemnation thereby incurred. Redemption is needed because of the bondage which sin has produced. Reconciliation to God we must have because one of the gravest effects of sin has been the way it has alienated us from God, producing utter estrangement of heart on our side. The word "alienated" occurs in Colossians 1:21, where it stands in full contrast to the fact that we now have been reconciled. We shall better understand the fulness of the reconciliation if we begin by grasping the full tragedy of the alienation.

One other passage refers to the state of alienation into which man has fallen — Ephesians 4:18. We get right to the bottom of things when we discover that we have been "alienated from the life of God." Connected with this alienation are such things as vanity, darkness, ignorance, blindness, lasciviousness, uncleanness. This is not surprising for the life of God is the exact opposite of all these things. Sin, having alienated us from God, has cut us off from all the things that go to make up life according to Him.

Alienated from God, we have naturally no desire for Him, nor for the light and life that His presence brings. This came out most clearly directly sin had entered and the alienation had come to pass. Genesis 3 bears witness to it; the action of Adam and his wife plainly declared it. Directly the voice of the Lord God was heard in the garden they hid themselves. God did not instantly destroy them. He dealt with them in mercy; still they had erected a barrier between themselves and Him which nothing on their side could surmount, and which He ratified by placing a barrier on His side in the shape of cherubim and a flaming sword.

Sin thus spoiled the Divine pleasure in man. To say this puts the matter too mildly. We have only to turn on to Genesis 6 to find that, mankind having been given sufficient time in which to develop their sinful propensities, an utterly unbearable state of affairs was produced, so that, "it repented the Lord that He had made man on the earth, and it grieved Him at His heart." At the end of Genesis 2 everything, man included, was pronounced to be "very good." Once man had been very good in the Divine eye, now he was a perfect grief to contemplate. The alienation was complete.

And it was complete on man's side also. God had become as distasteful to man as man had become to God. The latter part of Romans 1 unfolds the dreadful story of man's alienation from God. The sunken state of mankind is attributable to this, "they did not like to retain God in their knowledge" (verse 28). Romans 3 corroborates this by telling us that, "there is none that seeketh after God." When we get to Romans 5 it is plainly stated that when the reconciliation reached us we were "enemies."

Here we must carefully draw a distinction. On our side the alienation was not only in life but in heart also. On God's side the alienation in life was felt far more acutely than ever we could feel it, but there was no alienation in heart. In other words while we as sinners hated God, He never hated us. Had He hated us He could have just damned us, and left it at that. Instead of which He has Himself made available for us the reconciliation; a reconciliation brought to pass at so great a cost as "the death of His Son."

The Lord Jesus came into the world in the spirit of reconciliation. "God was in Christ, reconciling the world unto Himself, not imputing their trespasses unto them" (2 Cor. 5:19). This characterized His life and ministry. Not judgement but forgiveness was His work; and even where guilt was most pronounced and manifest, He did not impute it: see for instance John 8:11, and Luke 23:34. All that God could do was done by Him, yet every overture was rejected by men and He was crucified. But it was just then that God's reconciling mercy registered its most signal triumph.

Then it was that God "made Him to be sin for us, who knew no sin; that we might be made the righteousness of God in Him." Now it is evident that if we are made in Christ — in the Christ who died and rose again — the very righteousness of God, there can be no longer before Him that which is obnoxious and distasteful to Him. It cannot be any longer a grief to His heart to look down upon us, but the exact reverse. Christ was identified with us and our sin under the judgment of God. We are identified with Him and His acceptance as risen from the dead.

In Colossians 1:21, 22, the same truth is stated, but in other words. We have been reconciled "in the body of His flesh through death", for He became a Man, thereby possessing Himself of the body of His flesh, in order that He might die. As the result of reconciliation we can now be presented "holy and unblameable and unreproveable in His sight".

"In the body of His flesh" may seem a rather peculiar expression, but a similar form of words occurs elsewhere; Romans 7:4; Ephesians 2:15; Hebrews 10:10 and 20. If we understand the matter aright, the thought is that the Lord Jesus in His grace identified Himself with our place and condition in assuming Manhood apart from sin, so that He might lay down His life, presenting His sacred body as a sacrifice for sin; and then take up life again in resurrection, in which life believers may now be identified with Him. His death was thus the judgment and judicial ending of the old order; His resurrection the real beginning of the new.

This mighty change then has been brought about for us "in the body of His flesh through death"; and consequently our whole standing before God is manifestly altered. Once we were exactly in the position of fallen Adam, and nothing could be worse than that, nothing more repugnant to God. Now, being in Christ, we have the position that is Christ's as risen from the dead, and nothing could be better, nothing more delightful, more pleasing to God than that. This is what we may call God's side of reconciliation; the work which He has Himself effected in the death of Christ. It is perfect and absolute; accomplished for us, accomplished for ever. It is work of a new creation order, as 2 Corinthians 5:17 shows.

But there is our side of the matter which had equally to be met. It was we who were "alienated and enemies *in mind* by wicked works", and consequently there had to be a complete and fundamental change of mind and attitude as regards God with every one of us. There was no need that His heart should be turned towards us, but there was every need that our hearts should be turned towards Him. Hence the Gospel was committed to the Apostles as "the word of reconciliation". They carried on that ministry as "ambassadors for Christ", praying men "in Christ's stead, be ye reconciled to God" (2 Cor. 5:19, 20). When we believed the Gospel, the ministry of reconciliation became effective with us, and it could be said, "we have now received the reconciliation" (Rom. 5:11, margin). As the fruit of having received the reconciliation we "joy in God", whereas formerly we feared and even hated Him.

We may sum up, then, this most blessed truth by saying that everything about us which was obnoxious to God and deserving of judgment has been judged in the death of Christ; and as the fruit of reconciliation we stand in a perfect acceptance before Him. His work it is, for "He hath made us accepted in the Beloved" (Eph. 1:6). Christ's acceptance is the measure of our acceptance: and the measure of His acceptance may be discerned in the title given to Him — "the BELOVED". And further, since we do not believe the Gospel apart from the work of the Spirit in us, by which new birth is effected, we receive the reconciliation in believing. Our thoughts Godward are altogether altered; the enmity that once filled our hearts is removed, and we joy in Him. A new day has dawned in which He can look down upon us with complacency, and we look up in answering love to Him.

We can now see more clearly perhaps how reconciliation does carry us more fully into the positive blessings of the Gospel. As forgiven, we know that our sins have been dismissed. As justified, that we have been cleared from all charge. As redeemed, that our days of slavery are over. But as reconciled, we have full entrance into the wealth of the favour and love of God. It is the introduction into blessing of the highest order.

An old hymn states the matter thus:
"My God is reconciled,
His pardoning voice I hear."
That is hardly in keeping with what we have been seeing, is it?

It is not. It was we who needed to be reconciled. It was God who did the reconciling through the Lord Jesus Christ. But though this is so, we must not overlook the fact that God had to be propitiated in regard to sin. The publican of our Lord's parable knew this, for he said, "God be merciful [propitiated] to me a sinner" (Luke 18:13). God had to be propitiated inasmuch as sin was an outrageous challenge to His righteousness and holiness. He never hated us however. His heart was not estranged from man, for had it been He would never have sent His Son to be the propitiation, which was needed to meet the claims of His righteousness and holiness.

Do we understand then that reconciliation has more to do with our state before God than with the guilt of our sins?

It certainly has. It is worthy of note how the fact of our enmity comes into view when reconciliation is in question. The passage in 2 Corinthians 5 is an exception to this, but even here enmity, though not mentioned, is inferred, for it says, "old things are passed away; behold, all things are become new". Old things are passed away wherever new creation comes to pass, though they are very much in evidence in the world at present. As new-creation beings we are reconciled to God. Nevertheless we must not overlook the fact that "the blood of His cross" is the basis of the reconciliation, for it was there that sin met its judgment, and everything in us that was offensive and obnoxious to God was condemned. Our guilt is not overlooked, but even here it is more a question of the judgment of our sinful state than the expiation of our innumerable sins.

Why then, in Hebrews 2:17, do we read of Christ as "a merciful and faithful High Priest in things pertaining to God, to make reconciliation for the sins of the people"?

Simply because the translators of the Authorized Version inserted here the wrong word. It is "to make *propitiation* for the sins of the people", as the Revised and other versions show. Under the law Aaron the high priest made atonement by sprinkling the blood of the sacrifice on the mercyseat. The Lord Jesus has fulfilled the type, but on an infinitely grander scale. It is an interesting fact that in the Old Testament the word for "mercy-seat" is one closely allied to the word for *atonement;* whereas the word in the New Testament is as closely allied to *propitiation.* This shews that the propitiation of the New Testament embodies the idea of atonement, yet going beyond it. Reconciliation is to be distinguished from both, though not to be disconnected from either.

We have been dwelling on the fact that believers are reconciled now. What about the reconciliation of all things, spoken of in Colossians 1:20?

That far-reaching reconciliation is coming in its season. You will notice that the verse limits the blessing to "things in earth, or things in heaven". The "things under the earth", of Philippians 2:10, who are to bow at the name of Jesus, are not mentioned here. The blight of sin has affected certain parts of the heavens, through the fall of angelic beings. Wherever sin has been, there reconciliation is needed. A time is coming in which all that is evil will be swept into the place of judgment, there to lie under God's fiery indignation; and then all things purged and reconciled both on earth and in heaven will be delightful to God, and themselves delight in God.

The blood of His cross, that has already brought us into reconciliation, has power and value to accomplish even this.

There seems to be a sense in which the world is already reconciled, according to Romans 11:15. What does that passage mean?

The whole passage has to be read and carefully considered if we would arrive at the Apostle's thought. He is discussing God's ways with Israel as a nation, showing how they have been set aside for the present in order that He may pursue His purpose of extending mercy to Gentiles. Throughout the dispensation of law, God concentrated His favour and His dealings exclusively upon Israel: they were in the light of His countenance, and the nations were left in their darkness — the darkness which they had chosen for themselves, according to Romans 1:21. But with the advent of Christ and His rejection by Israel a great change in God's ways came to pass. Israel is fallen from their place of national favour, and this has led to what is called "the riches of the world", in verse 12, and to "the reconciling of the world" in verse 15.

The "world" here has evidently the force of the Gentile world as distinguished from Israel. The reconciling has been brought to pass by the change in God's dealings which has led Him to set Israel aside from their special place of national favour, and to bring the Gentile world before Him for blessing. Formerly the position was that the Gentiles had deliberately turned their faces from God, and He had turned His from them. Now He has turned toward them; and as Paul elsewhere said, "The salvation of God is sent unto the Gentiles, and . . . they will hear it" (Acts 28:28). This dispensational reconciliation has taken place and Paul was the chosen servant, sent to offer salvation to the Gentile world.

Does the reconciliation which we receive today involve more than this?

Most evidently it does. When we receive it we "joy in God", as we are told in Romans 5:11. This is a thing which the world cannot do, in spite of the fact that the mercy of God is active towards it in connection with the Gospel. When God gave His only-begotten Son He had the world in view, and love to the world was behind the gift. This dispensational reconciliation brings to all the ministry of reconciliation, of which 2 Corinthians 5 speaks; and that is not dispensational but intensely vital. Believers are really brought to God in righteousness and love, with every stain and discord removed, and every fear banished for ever.

Chapter Five

SALVATION

We now come to a word of very large meaning, so large indeed that it may be used in a sense that covers other gospel words such as justification, redemption, reconciliation. An instance of the large meaning which may be attached to it is found in Hebrews 2:3, where the mighty intervention of God on man's behalf, which first began to be spoken by the Lord Himself, is spoken of as "so great *salvation*". In Acts 13:26, the Apostle Paul speaks of "the word of this *salvation*", using the term in just the same broad sense. So also in Ephesians 1:13, the whole deliverance which has reached us in all its parts, is summed up in that one word. The Gospel which announces that mighty deliverance is, "the Gospel of our *salvation*". It is with this large meaning that we use the word in the title of this book.

Salvation is largely spoken of in both Old and New Testaments. In the Old Testament it is nearly always salvation from *enemies* that is before us, as Zechariah, the father of John the Baptist, stated. In his prophecy he declared that the holy prophets, raised up since the world began, had said that Israel should be saved from their enemies and from the hand of all that hate them. (See Luke 1:70, 71.) The New Testament in its very first chapter speaks of Jesus saving "His people from their sins" (Matt. 1:21). This at once lifts the whole matter on to a much higher platform.

But, whether in the Old or the New, the very fact that salvation is offered infers that those to whom it is offered are in *peril* of some sort: they are in danger of perishing. Indeed in 1 Corinthians 1:18, the contrast is drawn between "them that *perish*", and "us which are *saved*"; and the same contrast in almost exactly the same words appears again in 2 Corinthians 2: 15: Again we read, "The Son of Man is come to seek and to save that which was *lost*" (Luke 19:10). "Lord save us: we perish", was the cry of the disciples when in the storm on the lake of Galilee. It was only a matter of temporal deliverance, but then it was only in view of temporal danger. Salvation and perishing are clearly directly opposed as to their meaning.

As guilty, we need forgiveness. As under condemnation, we need justification. As having lapsed into bondage, we need redemption. As enemies in our minds by wicked works, utterly alienated from God, we need reconciliation. As lost and perishing, it is salvation we need.

When we considered ourselves as guilty or condemned, we had a perfectly crisp and definite thought before our minds. We saw ourselves arraigned at the bar of God. We stood, as it were, in a criminal court, charged with our sins. The thought was equally definite when we thought of ourselves as being in bondage to sin and Satan, or as being alienated from God. Sin now appeared to us as a taskmaster on the one hand, and as a dark cloud, shutting us out from God, on the other.

But now we have to consider ourselves as lost, as threatened by innumerable dangers both present and future, and consequently in danger of perishing. We cannot deal with this matter in quite the same crisp way. But what we have lost in definiteness we have more than made up in largeness and breadth of thought. God's salvation is a deliverance from *every peril which in the past or present or future could possibly threaten us*.

Still, though there is this comprehensiveness of meaning about the word, we must not miss the fact that it always carries the thought of deliverance from peril; and inasmuch as sin lies at the root of every peril that threatens us, the New Testament very appropriately opens with salvation from *sins*. This salvation is not merely from the penalty of sins, but from the power of sins, and even from the love of them. The Gospel does not offer an exemption from sin's penalty while leaving us free to continue under the power of sin, or in the enjoyment of sin's temporary pleasures. Were it to do so, it would be no true salvation, for it would just encourage us to continue in sin: which God forbid!

Yet again and again we find in Scripture that salvation does mean exemption or deliverance from the wrath of God. The Gospel is "the

power of God unto *salvation*, to every one that believeth ... for the
wrath of God is revealed from heaven" (Rom. 1:16–18). A little later in
the same epistle we read, "We shall be *saved* from *wrath* through Him"
(5:9). Again we read, "God hath not appointed us to *wrath*, but to obtain
salvation by our Lord Jesus Christ" (1 Thess. 5:9). And yet again in 2
Thessalonians 2:12, 13, we find that salvation is put in direct contrast
with damnation.

The fact is that the Old Testament has as its chief theme the
dealings of God with Israel His people in view of the coming of the
Messiah. Hence the consequences of sin as regards God's *governmental*
actings are mainly in view. When Israel sinned, God in His government
brought up enemies against them, and when they repented He saved
them. The New Testament brings into view the *eternal* consequences of
sin, and the way in which every individual soul of man is subject to God's
judgment and the infliction of wrath from heaven. From that wrath we
are saved.

It is in this connection that salvation may be spoken of as a past
and completed thing, so that believers can speak of themselves as, "us,
which *are* saved". The Lord Jesus is our Deliverer from the wrath to
come, and we can never be more secure than we are today, before the
wrath actually falls. Yet when we speak of ourselves as saved the
emphasis seems mainly to lie on the fact that once we were engulfed in
every kind of evil and defilement and now we are rescued out of it all.
"We ourselves also were sometimes foolish, disobedient, deceived,
serving divers lusts and pleasures, living in malice and envy, hateful, and
hating one another. But ... He *saved* us" (Titus 3:3–5).

It is very evident however, that though we can speak of God as the
One who "*hath* saved us", (2 Tim. 1:9), we are still in a world that is full
of seductions, with the treacherous flesh within us, and Satan the astute
adversary without. Hence we need salvation daily — salvation of practically a continuous sort. Scripture speaks very plainly of this present salvation. The Lord Jesus is living in heaven as our High Priest to minister it
to us. He is able to "save them to the uttermost that come unto God by
Him, seeing He ever liveth to make intercession for them" (Heb. 7:25).

The present salvation, which we need and get as believers, is of
course based upon the death of Christ, but it actually reaches us by His

priestly activities on our behalf as He lives for us on high. We are being "saved by His life" (Rom. 5:10); and inasmuch as He ever lives we shall be saved to the uttermost. We shall be saved completely, to the extremest point of time; to the moment when the last foe has disappeared, and we are beyond the need of any further salvation for ever.

In order that we may enjoy this practical, everyday salvation we are granted the instruction which is furnished by the Word of God. The Holy Scriptures are able to make us "wise unto salvation through faith which is in Christ Jesus" (2 Tim. 3:15). The next verse speaks of the Scriptures being profitable not only for teaching but also "for reproof, for correction, for instruction in righteousness". This shows the kind of salvation that was in Paul's mind when he wrote, and emphasizes the great part which the Scriptures play in our daily salvation.

When Paul wrote these words he of course alluded to the Old Testament Scriptures, which Timothy had known from his childhood. They abound with salutary warnings for us, and if we heed them we shall be saved from a thousand snares and dangers. We need hardly add that what Paul asserts of the Old Testament is equally true of the New, which some of us have been privileged to know from our youth.

We might sum up the matter as regards this daily and present salvation by saying it is ours as the result of Christ's High Priestly intercession, and of our having the Word of God, coupled with the possession of the Holy Spirit, whereby we may understand it and accept its instructions and its warnings.

There remains a further group of Scriptures that clearly speak of salvation as a future thing. It is our hope, and is to be worn "for an helmet" (1 Thess. 5:8). Our hope of salvation will be realized at the second advent of Christ. It is true that He is coming as the Judge, but we do not look for Him in that character. For us it is written, "We look for the *Saviour* . . . who shall change our vile body, that it may be fashioned like unto His glorious body" (Phil. 3:20, 21). Hence it is that we are left here to "look for Him" when He shall "appear the second time, without sin, unto *salvation*" (Heb. 9:28).

This future salvation altogether depends upon the crowning act of mercy which will reach us as the last delivering act of the Lord Jesus on our behalf. It will involve the raising of the dead saints, and the catching

away of the living saints before the full storm of God's righteous wrath
breaks on the earth. Then all of us — both dead and living — are to be
found for ever with Christ in bodies of glory like to His own. This will
be the final thing. Salvation as regards ourselves will be absolutely
completed.

> The Philippians were bidden by Paul, "Work out
> your own salvation with fear and trembling." How
> do you reconcile this injunction with what we have
> had before us?

A long passage leads up to this injunction. If we want to get an idea
of the context we have to go back as far as verse 27 of chapter 1. The
Philippian believers were threatened by adversaries without and dissen-
sion within. The close of chapter 1 alludes to the one. The opening of
chapter 2 alludes to the other. The former is easily disposed of: to meet
the latter the whole weight of the matchless example of Christ has to be
brought in. And then the Apostle himself was no longer present for their
help, for he was in a Roman prison.

Under these circumstances they were to show their spiritual mettle
and work out their salvation from the threatening dangers: but not as
being cast upon their own resources, for "it is God which worketh in you
both to will and to do of His good pleasure" (verse 13). If the next three
verses were fulfilled in them, they would indeed have worked out their
salvation.

A present, daily salvation is in question: and our side of the matter
is emphasized here. The Divine side must come first — the Priesthood of
Christ, the work of God in us by His spirit, the instruction and correction of His Word. But the human side has its importance. We have to
diligently avail ourselves of the grace that God provides.

On the day of Pentecost Peter exhorted the
anxious enquirers saying, "Save yourselves from
this untoward generation;" and those who received
his word were baptized. In his first Epistle he again
speaks of baptism as saving us. What is this
salvation which baptism effects?

It is salvation from "this untoward generation", as Peter said.
Another translation puts it, "Be saved from this perverse generation."
Now baptism is, in one word, *dissociation*. It is only an outward ordinance, yet it has a meaning: and that is its meaning. It is based upon the
death and resurrection of Christ, for we are "baptized into His death"
(Rom. 6:3), and so we are "buried with Him" (Col. 2:12). Nothing more
effectively dissociates us from the present order of things, cutting our
links with the world, than death and burial.

The particular point that Peter makes, both in his sermon and his
epistle, is that baptism cut the link between the repentant and believing
Jews and the unrepentant and unbelieving mass of that nation. That lies
upon the surface of Acts 2, and is involved, we believe, in 1 Peter 3:21; for
his epistle was addressed to believing Jews. He tells them that baptism is
a "like figure" unto the waters of the flood that of old cut the link
between believing Noah with his house and the world of the ungodly.
Noah and his house had been saved "by" or "through" the water from
the ruin and death that came in upon the godless earth. Those to whom
Peter wrote had been saved through baptism from the godless mass of
their nation. They suffered much from the ungodly mass but they were
saved from their fate, whether in this life, at the destruction of Jerusalem,
or in the world to come.

When a big ship is sinking, it is not enough to let down small boats
by ropes and then get into them. Unless the ropes are cut there will be no
salvation. Baptism cuts the ropes, and in that sense saves.

"He that shall endure unto the end the same shall
be saved." In the light of this is it not premature to
speak of ourselves as saved, while we are still on
our way to the end?

It certainly would be, if these words of our Lord referred to the way in which sinful men might receive the salvation of their souls. These words however, which occur in the course of His prophetic discourse recorded in Matthew 24, and Mark 13, do not refer to that. The Lord was not addressing sinners but men who already had been brought into relationships with Himself — His *disciples*. At that moment they were representative of the chosen remnant of Israel, who will be found on earth at the time of the end.

"The end" in this passage is not the end of this or that individual life, but the end of the whole time of persecution, trial and sorrow, which end will be brought about by the second coming of Christ. Endurance is the supreme virtue which is to mark these saints, for their salvation is sure when Christ appears.

That is the primary bearing of this passage; but there are of course many profitable applications of it which we may make for ourselves. However to apply it so as to teach that one cannot be really sure of salvation until one dies is not one of them.

Why is "confession with the mouth" so definitely connected with salvation in Romans 10:10?

Because salvation is a term of such wide meaning, and includes deliverance from the world, amongst other things. We believe on Christ as risen from the dead with our hearts, and that means our justification before God. Both these however — the faith and the justification — are not observable, for it is not so much a judicial fact as a practical fact — we are really saved from the power of world, flesh, and devil. The very first step towards a salvation of such a sort must be the confession of Christ as Lord, made with the mouth so that men may hear it. A silent confession of Christ in the mind — just thinking it — obviously would not do.

The distinction made in this passage between the faith of the heart leading to righteousness and the confession of the mouth leading to salvation is very striking. It greatly helps to show the special force of salvation.

Is that why Cornelius, God-fearing man though he was, needed Peter to come to him that he might be saved? He was told that Peter "shall tell thee words, whereby thou and all thy house shall be saved."

No doubt it was so. Until Peter arrived with the Gospel message concerning the risen Christ, Cornelius could not believe in his heart that God had raised Him from the dead. Again, if he had thought of Him in any sense as Lord, it would doubtless have been as Lord of the children of Israel. Peter preached Him in the house of Cornelius as "Lord of all".

Cornelius had turned from his heathenism to the fear of God very sincerely; but salvation came to him when he believed on and confessed the risen Christ as Lord.

You do not wish us to understand then that salvation is a higher order of Christian blessing into which we may come subsequent to conversion? — so that, for instance, a man might be forgiven yet not saved.

Such a deduction as that from the case of Cornelius would be quite unwarranted. Yet we must not miss the instruction conveyed by the fact that though he had the fear of God, and faith in Him, and even knew certain facts about Christ's ministry on earth, he was not saved until he heard and believed the glad tidings of the risen Christ and forgiveness in His Name. Then it was that he was delivered clean out of the old world system which had held him and was brought to God.

Almost all that we have been considering is in connection with what we are saved from. What are we saved to?

We are saved to every blessing that is ours in Christ. And yet, if we carefully follow Scripture phraseology, salvation is mostly, if not always, connected with what we are delivered from; and if it is a question of what we are brought to the word used is *"calling"*. God has "saved us, and called us with an holy calling" (2 Tim. 1:9).

Israel was saved out of Egypt in order that they might enjoy the land to which God called them. We are saved from the world, the flesh, the devil, and the wrath of God which is to come, in order that we may enjoy God's call to the place of sons and share the coming glory of Christ. The salvation which is ours in Christ is a very mighty and wonderful thing; and thereby we are liberated to enjoy our calling. Yet all those things to which we are called according to the sovereign purpose of God are more wonderful still.

Chapter Six

———————

SANCTIFICATION

The Scriptures have a good deal to say to us as to sanctification, in the Old Testament as well as in the New; and wherever we find it the word has the fundamental meaning of a *separation*, or a *setting apart*. In the Old Testament the word is freely used of things as well as persons. In the New Testament it is mainly, though not exclusively, used of persons; and as applying to believers it has a double significance — a primary meaning and a secondary. The trouble with so many is that the secondary meaning has obliterated the primary in their minds. Hence the difficulties which they feel in relation to this important subject.

The sanctification of believers means to many people, perhaps to most, a process by which they are made more and more holy and pleasing to God; whereas its primary meaning is that by an act of God they have been set apart for Himself, and according to this their growth in holiness becomes a necessity.

The root idea of the word then, whether we take its Old or New Testament use, is that of setting apart for God. A sanctified person or thing is one set apart from ordinary uses to be for God's own possession and use and enjoyment. In contradistinction to sanctification stands *profanation*. The priest of Aaron's time was not to "defile himself ... to profane himself" (Lev. 21:4). The priests of the coming millennial day are to "teach My people the difference between the holy and profane" (Ezek. 44:24). The very word used there means "common or polluted", and of course it is just when a thing is put to common use that it does get polluted. That is easily seen in connection with the ordinary affairs of life. When a piece of ground is thrown open freely to the public it becomes a "common", and at once rules must be made to keep it decent. Left to itself it would soon become more or less of a rubbish heap.

In the primary sense of the word, every believer *has been* set apart for God. It is a fact of an absolute nature. We may speak of it as *positional* sanctification.

In the secondary sense, every believer is to be set apart for God. It is not positional but *progressive* sanctification.

The primary is an *objective fact*: the secondary is a *subjective experience*, which must always follow and flow out of the objective fact. Things are bound to get out of place and distorted in our minds, if we allow the subjective experience to eclipse the objective fact, as so many do.

If any of our readers are inclined to doubt what we have just laid down as to the primary meaning of the word, let them consider three facts.

(1) Inanimate things — altar, laver, vessels — were sanctified under the law. There could be no subjective change, no increase in holiness, in them. But they could be put in a separate *position*, wholly devoted to the service of God.

(2) The Lord Jesus Himself was "sanctified, and sent into the world" (John 10:36); and again leaving the world He said, "I sanctify Myself" (John 17:19). There could be no subjective change in Him — no sanctification in the progressive sense. Holiness of the most intense order, divine and absolute, was ever His. But He could be set apart by the Father for His mission as Revealer and Redeemer, and then sent into the world. Also, as leaving this world and entering the world of the Father's glory, He could set Himself apart in a new *position* as the pattern and power of the sanctification of His followers.

(3) The instruction comes to us, "Sanctify the Lord God in your hearts" (1 Peter 3:15). Here too the only possible sense of "sanctify", is to set apart positionally. In our hearts we are to set the Lord God apart in the *position* altogether unique. He is to be exalted without a rival there.

Now as to ourselves we have to begin with this absolute and positional sanctification which is ours by the act of God. If we do not, we are sure to get defective, if not perverted, ideas of the practical and progressive sanctification which is to be ours, since the one flows out of the other. The practical sanctification expected is according to the character of the positional sanctification conferred.

The first mention of sanctification in the Bible is in connection with creation, when God sanctified the seventh day in which He rested (Gen. 2:3); the second is in connection with redemption, when He brought Israel out of Egypt. Here persons were in question, for He said, "Sanctify unto Me all the firstborn" (Ex. 13:2). Those who had been redeemed by blood were set apart for God positionally, and because they were, a very special manner of life became them, or rather became the Levites, who later on were substituted for them (see Num. 3:45; 8:5–19).

The type, with which the book of Exodus furnishes us, is a very instructive one. In chapter 12 the children of Israel are sheltered from judgment by the blood of the lamb, which foreshadows the forgiveness and justification which reaches us by the Gospel. In chapter 15 they are brought right out of Egypt, the power of Pharaoh being broken, which illustrates salvation. Both chapters together foreshadow redemption. But in chapter 13 we get sanctification. The people justified by blood are set apart for God; and because He claims them for Himself, He will brook no rival claim. He made good His claim against Pharaoh's claim. He broke the might Egypt and, delivering His people, He brought them to Himself. All their later history had to be governed by this fact.

In all this God showed very plainly that when He intended to bless a people He would set them apart for Himself, instead of allowing them to be common, polluted, profaned. They were sanctified to Himself.

How utterly man has been profaned by sin! His mind, his heart, the whole course of nature with him, has overrun with every kind of evil. If grace sets itself to win him, he must, in the very nature of things, be set apart for God.

We begin then by laying hold of the great fact that we have been sanctified. Scripture is very definite and plain as to this point, and perhaps the most striking example it furnishes us with is the case of the Corinthians. Of all the Christians of the apostolic age, that we have any knowledge of, they stand out as the least marked by sanctification of a practical sort. Their behaviour was open to much censure, and they got it from the Apostle Paul in very plain language. Yet in his first epistle to them he calls them "saints", as "sanctified in Christ Jesus" (1:2). Later in the same epistle, after mentioning many of the abominations that filled the heathen world, he said, "And such were some of you: but . . . ye are sanctified" (6:11).

Nothing could be clearer than this. We do not become God's sanctified people by attaining to a certain standard of practical holiness. We are God's sanctified ones, and because of it, holiness, or practical sanctification, is incumbent upon us. If the former were God's way it would be according to the very principle of law. The latter is God's way and it is according to the principle of grace.

This absolute sanctification reaches us in a two-fold way. In the first place it is by the work of Christ. "We are sanctified through the offering of the body of Jesus Christ once for all" (Heb. 10:10). "Jesus also, that He might sanctify the people with His own blood, suffered without the gate" (Heb. 13:12). Believing in Him, we stand in the value of His offering and are thereby set apart for God just as fully as we are justified.

In the second place we are sanctified by the Holy Spirit. To the Thessalonians Paul wrote in his second epistle, "God hath from the beginning chosen you to salvation through sanctification of the Spirit and belief of the truth" (2:13). Peter also wrote in his first epistle, "Elect . . . through sanctification of the Spirit" (1:2). There are the workings of the Spirit in our hearts, culminating in the new birth of which we read in John 3, when "that which is born of the Spirit is spirit". Then further, when the Gospel is received in faith the Spirit indwells the believer, sealing him until the day of redemption. By that seal the believer is marked off as belonging to God: he is sanctified as set apart for Him.

To the Corinthians Paul wrote in his first epistle, "Christ Jesus, who of God is made unto us . . . sanctification" (1:30). We are set apart in Him, inasmuch as His was the blood shed for us, and also we have received the Spirit as the fruit of His work. We, as well as the Corinthians, have been, "sanctified . . . in the name of the Lord Jesus, and by the Spirit of our God" (6:11).

When once we have laid hold of the fact that we have been sanctified in this absolute sense we are prepared to face our responsibilities as to practical sanctification, which are based upon it. One of the requests for His own, uttered by the Lord, as recorded in John 17 was, "Sanctify them through Thy truth: Thy Word is truth." Hence the importance of giving all due heed to the Word of God, for the more we really know it the more its sanctifying power is exerted in our lives.

"This is the will of God, even your sanctification," is what Paul wrote to the Thessalonians (4:3), showing that it is not something that is optional for the Christian, something to be pursued or avoided as fancy dictates. Moreover God Himself works it out for His saints, and it is all-embracing in its scope, for Paul went on to pray for them, "The very God of peace sanctify you wholly" (5:23). Everything about us is to come under the sanctifying touch of the God of peace.

But, on the other hand, there is our side of the matter. There are measures which we are to take for the promotion of it. We are to "shun" certain things; we are to "depart from iniquity"; we are to "purge" ourselves from vessels unto dishonour, who teach error of a sort that overthrows faith; then we may be vessels "unto honour, sanctified, and meet for the Master's use" (2 Tim. 2:21).

In all these ways the practical work of sanctification progresses. Indeed it is the great work which the Lord is carrying on with His church; His object being to "sanctify and cleanse it with the washing of water by the Word" (Eph. 5:26). The work of sanctification and cleansing is taking place today in the individuals of whom the church is composed.

Again and again in the Scriptures we are exhorted to holiness. What is the difference between this and the sanctification we have been considering?

There is no real difference. The same Greek word is translated by both English words, and like sanctification holiness is spoken of (1) as positional and absolute, and (2) as practical and progressive. For instance, when we read, "Wherefore holy brethren, partakers of the heavenly calling . . ." (Heb. 3:1), we are not to understand this to mean that they were far advanced in practical holiness, but that they were a people set apart for God as partaking in the heavenly calling. Chapter 5, verses 11–14, indicate that they were not very far advanced, and presently we find that they are exhorted to "follow peace with all men, and holiness" (12:14), which infers the same thing. The *holy* brethren are to *follow holiness.* In the first epistle of Peter we find just the same thing. He says, *"Be ye holy"* (1:15) to the very people to whom he says, "Ye are ... an holy nation" (2:9).

Because we are holy we are to be holy. The holiness, which is to characterize us practically, is according to the holiness which is ours by the call of God.

Believers in Christ are frequently called "saints" in the New Testament. Is the popular use of this term in keeping with the Scriptural use?

By no means. A "saint" is popularly supposed to be an eminently holy person. The Romish authorities still make saints by a lengthy process called "canonization". If we lived amongst Romanists and spoke of "going to visit the saints" they would probably imagine we are going to visit some local shrine and invoke the aid from the spirit world of some of these canonized people. And many who are not Romanists have not quite shaken off these ideas. A saint is not a person of unusual piety, who after death is entitled to be represented in effigy or picture with a halo round his or her head, but the ordinary, simple believer — each one who has been set apart for God by the blood of Christ, and by the possession of the Holy Spirit.

Every true believer being a saint means that we each are responsible to pursue holiness. Perhaps one reason why the Romish idea lingers so strongly is that it leads people to feel that holiness is no particular concern of theirs, but only of a few. These special ones may pursue holiness; the rest of us can live easy-going lives in the world!

Let us be careful to maintain the scriptural thought.

Do justification and sanctification go together?

They do, as far as positional sanctification is concerned. In 1 Corinthians 6:11, where the work wrought "in the name of the Lord Jesus, and by the Spirit of our God", is in question, sanctification is mentioned even in advance of justification. The Corinthians had been cleansed and set apart for God on the same ground and by the same agency as they had been justified, and so also have we.

Seeing that they do go together, are we right in speaking of sanctification by faith, just as we speak of justification by faith?

We have in Scripture the definite statement that we are "justified by faith" (Rom. 5:1), but we do not anywhere read that we are sanctified by faith. Nevertheless, just as, having been justified, we know it by faith and not by our feelings, so too we know that we have been set apart for God by faith and not by feelings. God declares us to be justified as believers in Jesus, and we believe Him. He declares us to be sanctified to Himself as believers in Jesus, and again we believe Him.

If practical sanctification be in question it is another matter. That is progressive, and there should be increase in it to the end. We are to be "perfecting holiness in the fear of God" (2 Cor. 7:1), and Paul prayed for the Thessalonians to the end that they might be sanctified "unto the coming of our Lord Jesus Christ". Holiness is not, of course, *apart from* faith, but to speak of holiness by faith, as though faith alone produced it, is to shut out elements of Christian living which ought by no means to be excluded.

What then are these elements? How is practical sanctification or holiness produced?

In the latter part of Romans 6, holiness is presented as being the "fruit" of our being emancipated from the slavery of sin. Now it is "the law of the Spirit of life in Christ Jesus" which makes us "free from the law of sin and death" (Rom. 8:2). The more we are under the law, or control, of the Spirit the more do we enjoy freedom from the control of sin. Evidently therefore *the control of the Holy Spirit* is a very important element in practical sanctification.

Again, when the Lord was praying for His own, as recorded in John 17, He said, "Sanctify them through Thy truth: Thy word is truth" (verse 17). The Spirit of God and the Word of God are intimately connected. They were in creation, as the first three verses of Genesis 1 show. They are together also in the new birth, and again in the matter of practical sanctification. We can speak of *holiness* by the *Word of truth* as well as of *holiness by the Spirit*.

We can also speak of *holiness by love* in the light of 1 Thessalonians 3:12–13. As love increases so are our hearts established in holiness.

And yet again there is *holiness by separation from all that is unclean*, coupled with cleansing from all filthiness of flesh and spirit. 2 Corinthians 6:14–17:1 tells us this. And 2 Timothy 2:16–22 tells us the same thing, but in a somewhat different setting.

Here then are four elements in addition to faith by which holiness is produced.

We sometimes meet those who speak of being "wholly sanctified", in a way that suggests a claim to entire freedom from the presence of sin. Is there any support for this in the Bible?

There is verse 23 of 1 Thessalonians 5, to which we have already referred. But the context shows that the word, "wholly" refers to the whole man in his tripartite nature — "spirit and soul and body." There is nothing partial about God's gracious work. Its sanctifying influence reaches every part of us, and is carried on "unto the coming of our Lord Jesus Christ." When He comes the sanctification of the whole man will be carried to its completeness and perfection; but not before.

As long as we inhabit these bodies, derived from Adam, sin is still in us; yet the more we experience God's sanctifying work the less we come under its power. There is no excuse for the believer when he sins, inasmuch as ample power is at his disposal to preserve him. Yet we *all* often offend, as James has told us in his Epistle; and we shall *all* confess it, unless our sense of what is sin is sadly blunted, or we are just deceiving ourselves.

A life of practical holiness is indeed proper and normal Christian life; but the one who most lives it talks least about himself. The end of his living and the theme of his tongue is CHRIST.

Chapter Seven

———————

THE NEW BIRTH

We are introduced to this theme by the Lord Himself, who put it in the very forefront of His teaching when He had the talk with Nicodemus by night. It is alluded to by John in the preface to his Gospel (1:13), but not in any way expounded until we come to chapter 3. Having heard of it more fully from the lips of the Lord, we find further details as to it both in 1 Peter and 1 John. We also discover from what the Lord says to Nicodemus that Ezekiel 36 alludes to it, though the term, "born again," is not used there.

Nicodemus was amongst those who were convinced that Jesus was "a teacher come from God", but he went further than the men spoken of at the end of chapter 2, by becoming an enquirer. Nicodemus himself was "a master (*i.e.* teacher) of Israel", and it was something that he should recognize in Jesus a Teacher, who spoke and acted with an authority far above his own. But recognizing it, he came as one who would make a very good scholar, being a privileged person, a member of the most favoured nation. To such a man as this the pronouncement was made that, "Except a man be born again, he cannot see the kingdom of God."

The word translated "again", in this passage has also the meaning of "from above"; it is so translated in John 3:31, and elsewhere; but evidently Nicodemus did not understand it in this sense, or he would hardly have asked the question recorded in verse 4. In Luke 1:3 the same word is translated, "from the very first", and that seems to be the force of it here. Nicodemus needed a birth which should be new in the very beginnings of its origin. Nothing short of that would do.

He had been born of the stock of Abraham, and so his pedigree was of the best. He was a very fine specimen of the Abrahamic strain of humanity, yet he would not do for God. The Lord's words clearly put the sentence of condemnation upon him as a child of Abraham, for if that first birth had sufficed there would have been no need for a new one. We Gentiles cannot boast of being children of Abraham, the friend of God: we are just the children of Adam, the man who disobeyed and fell. The new birth cannot be less necessary for us than it was for Nicodemus. He too, of course, was a child of Adam, just as Abraham was.

Adam's nature was corrupted by his sin, and all his race, generation after generation, partake of that fallen and corrupt nature. Spiritual blindness is one of the forms that the corruption takes, and so we are quite unable to "see the kingdom of God". When Jesus was on earth the kingdom was present amongst men, for He was the King; but men did not see this apart from the new birth. Nicodemus only saw a Teacher in Him, and needed to be born again to see Him in the true light. It is just the same today though Jesus is no longer here. Men see in Him a religious Teacher or a Reformer, but they do not see God in Him, nor do they see the kingdom of God, unless they have come under that Divinely wrought process of cleansing which the new birth involves.

In verse 5 of chapter 3, the Lord carries His teaching a step further. We need not only to see the kingdom but to enter it, and for this we must be born "of water and of the Spirit". The water is the agent employed, and the Spirit the Actor who employs it. These further statements apparently only puzzled Nicodemus the more, and he asked incredulously, "How can these things be?" The Lord's reply took also the form of a question, "Art thou a master of Israel, and knowest not these things?" His teaching on this point was not something entirely new — unheard of up to this point. It had its roots in what the prophets had testified, and notably Ezekiel in his thirty-sixth chapter, where both water and the Spirit are mentioned. The surprising thing was that Nicodemus had remained in ignorance of the prophet's meaning.

The meaning of the word, "water", in John 3 has been much in dispute. We believe its true meaning is to be discerned by referring back to the Scripture to which the Lord alluded. He doubtless used the word as being just that which ought to have put Nicodemus into possession of

the key which should unlock His meaning. We ought to read at this point
Ezekiel 36:21–33.

Having read it, we note that the passage speaks of what the Lord
will do when at last He gathers Israel His people out of the lands of their
dispersion and brings them into their own land. Then He will sprinkle
"clean water" upon them and they shall be clean. All their filthiness and
their love of idols shall be gone, for He will thereby have put "a new
heart" and "a new spirit" within them. The cleansing effected by the
water will be of so radical and fundamental a nature that their whole
nature will be different. Once this mighty work has taken place they will
look back on that which formerly they were with disgust — "Then shall
ye remember your own ways, and your doings that were not good,
and shall lothe yourselves in your own sight for your iniquities and
for your abominations" (verse 31). A moral renovation will have been
accomplished.

By discarding bad habits and acquiring good habits, men sometimes achieve a considerable measure of that kind of moral alteration
which lies on the surface. The moral *renovation* which Ezekiel predicts
goes down to the deepest foundation; putting a man into possession of a
new heart and a new spirit, so that instinctively he desires what is good
and walks in obedience. Verse 27 shows this. No wonder then that the
Lord Jesus spoke of it as a new birth; inasmuch as it is not the altering of
a nature already existing, but the impartation of a nature which is entirely
new. The new heart is *"given"*. The new spirit is *"put within you"*. It is to
start anew from the very first.

Verse 27 speaks of "My Spirit" which is to be put within born-
again Israel in that day. Though not printed with a capital in our Bibles, it
clearly should be, as it refers to the Spirit of God, and hence is to be distinguished from "a new spirit" in the previous verse. So the prophet
clearly shows us that only when Israel is born again and receives the
Spirit of God will they see and enter into the kingdom of God.

All this Nicodemus should have known, though the Lord's words
to him carry the truth concerning it a good deal further. Now we
discover that new birth is actually produced by the Spirit of God. He
who is born again is born of the Spirit, and that which is born of the
Spirit is spirit as to its own nature and character. In other words, the new

heart and new spirit, of which Ezekiel tells us, is the product of the Holy Spirit and partakes of His holy nature. That which is born of the flesh is flesh, in spite of all that may be done to it in the way of refinement, education, civilization, or Christianization. When all is done, flesh it still remains: it cannot be transmuted into spirit. That alone is spirit which is born of the Spirit. It cannot be found apart from the new birth.

When Ezekiel prophesied of how God would "sprinkle clean water" upon Israel in the coming day in order that they might be clean, the mind of those who read his words would have been carried back to the book of Numbers where twice we get the sprinkling of water mentioned. In chapter 8 we get the way in which the Levites were cleansed in order that they might enter upon their service. Moses was told to "Sprinkle water of purifying upon them". In chapter 19 we get the way in which the ordinary Israelite was cleansed from various defilements which he might contract. From the ashes of a red heifer "a water of separation" was to be made, and that water was to be sprinkled upon people and things that were defiled. The "water of separation" which purified was made from "the ashes of the burnt heifer" — typical of the death of Christ — and "running [or, living] water" — typical of the Spirit.

So we pass from the type in Numbers to the prophecy in Ezekiel, and from thence to the Lord's declaration in John 3. Putting all together the significance of the "water" begins to appear. It is the Word of God which brings the death of Christ in its separating and purifying power to bear upon the soul. Of that Word, as well as of the Spirit, we must be born if we are to enter the kingdom of God. In later chapters of the Gospel we find the Lord connecting water with His Word in a way that confirms the matter. Compare the scene recorded in chapter 13:5–11, with His words, "Now ye are clean through the word which I have spoken unto you" (15:3). A further confirmation occurs in Ephesians 5:26, where "water" and "the Word" are brought together as identical.

Man needs, then, to be born anew from the very beginning. The agent used for this is the Word of God, which applies to us the cleansing virtue of the death of Christ. And He who acts in this matter is the Spirit of God. In John 3 the water is mentioned but once: the remainder of the instruction concerns the action of the Spirit.

But when we turn to 1 Peter 1:22–25, we find that though the Spirit is mentioned, the main emphasis lies upon that which the water symbolizes — the Word of God. We have obeyed the truth by the Spirit, and thereby purification has reached us — verse 22 views that which is accomplished from our side. Verses 23–25 view it from God's side. The purification is effective by reason of His work in us by His Word, which, as we know from John 3, is wrought by the Spirit. We are born "by" the Word, but also "of" incorruptible seed; and we must not confuse these two things. "By" indicates *agency*; "of" indicates *origin*.

As children of Adam we were born of seed which is not merely corruptible but actually and fatally *corrupted*. We are born again of seed which is *incorruptible*, because Divine. Isaiah the prophet was given a glimpse of the Servant of Jehovah, who should die and rise again; and he predicted, "When Thou shalt make His soul an offering for sin, He shall see *His seed*" (53:10). He shall see those who take their spiritual origin from Himself. A thought akin to this seems to lie in these words in Peter. As born again we have a new origin which is incorruptible in nature; and the Word by which we are born again, "liveth and abideth for ever". That which is produced as the result of new birth is characterized by these wonderful things — *life, eternity* and *incorruptibility*.

From all that we have seen it is very evident that new birth is that work of the Spirit of God in us which is necessitated by the corruption of our nature through sin. It was not enough that a work should be wrought for us which should bring us justification and reconciliation; there must also be this work of moral cleansing, this lifting us out of the corruption of our nature. No external work of cleansing would meet the case; nothing short of our becoming possessed of a new nature springing from an incorruptible source. No deeper or more fundamental purification than that could be conceived.

From the passage in Peter, with its statement as to our being born of incorruptible seed, we pass on naturally to 1 John, where we read, "Whosoever is born of God doth not commit sin; for His seed remaineth in him: and he cannot sin, because he is born of God" (3:9). This verse gives us perhaps the fullest development of the whole matter. No mention is made of the agent employed, the Word of God. Nor is the Spirit of God, who acts in the work, mentioned. The emphasis is concentrated upon God Himself as the Source of all. As born of God, His seed remains in us; it is irrevocable. And we partake of His sinless nature. The born again one cannot sin, just because he is born of God.

In so speaking John views us abstractly, according to the essential character of the new nature which is ours. He is entitled to do so, inasmuch as when God has completed His work concerning us we shall be this not merely abstractly but absolutely. The last trace of the Adamic nature will be gone when our very bodies are glorified. Elsewhere John views us practically, and insists that we have sin in us, and that we do sin: see, 1:8–2:2. This practical view of things is very necessary of course; but so also is the abstract view, which we have before us. It is most important that we should know the sinlessness of the nature that is ours as born of God.

Not only is it *sinless* — for that is a negative virtue: it is also *righteous* (2:29), and *loving* (3:10, 11). It is marked by *faith* (5:1), and by *overcoming the world* (5:4). These are positive features of great worth. Only let these characteristics come clearly into display in the believer and it becomes manifest to all men that a mighty moral renovation has been effected: a thorough-going cleansing and purification has been accomplished indeed.

We read of cleansing by the blood of Christ in 1 John 1:7. Do you differentiate between this and the cleansing we have been considering? And, if so, how?

The blood of Christ signifies His holy life laid down in death for the bearing of the judgment due to us. Thereby we are cleansed *judicially*. The cleansing wrought by new birth and presented as accomplished by water, touches our characters, and involves our having a new nature. We are cleansed *morally*. We could not do without either. Both are ours as having received the grace of God.

You do not think then that the "water", in John 3, has anything to do with baptism?

We are sure that the Lord did not allude to baptism in using the word "water". There would have been nothing surprising in Nicodemus not knowing about it, had that been His meaning. No, He alluded to Ezekiel 36, which Nicodemus ought to have known, and that has nothing to do with baptism. John 3:5 has no more to do with baptism than John 6:53 has to do with the Lord's supper: though in both cases we may be able to discern in the out-ward ordinances some reflection of the truth stated in these passages. In both cases however we have not the ordinance but *the truth*, to which the ordinance makes some reference.

We have had before us different terms: "born again," "born of water and of the Spirit", "born of God". Do they all mean the same thing?

They all refer, we believe, to the same great work of God, wrought in us by His Spirit. There is no such thought in Scripture as there being two more different kinds of "new birth"; as though, for example, one might be "born again", according to John 3, and yet not "born of God", according to 1 John 3. On the other hand, each of these different expressions has its own significance and force. The first emphasizes the new and original character of the birth. The second, who accomplishes it, and the agent employed. The third, the Source whence all springs. Indeed we think an orderly progress of doctrine may be observed in the four passages, beginning with Ezekiel.

New birth is evidently an act of God; but is it wrought by the Spirit altogether apart from the preaching of the Gospel?

There is a plain answer to that question in the passage in Peter. It says, "Born again . . . by the word of God . . . and this is the word which by the gospel is preached unto you." Whatever may have been the word by which the Spirit worked in the past dispensation, in this day the word by which we are born again is that which reaches us in the Gospel.

Then are we born again by simply believing the
Gospel? Some hold that we believe to be born
again, others that we must be born again to believe.

That is so. He who inclines to Arminianism would hold the first
view. He who inclines to Calvinism would hold the second. This raises
the whole question of how to adjust in our minds the sovereignty of God
and the responsibility of man. We should answer the question by saying,
No, not by *simply* believing the Gospel; for, if by believing *only*, we
should be shutting out factors of even greater importance. But of course
we should be equally wrong if we said it was *simply* by the Spirit; for
then we should be shutting out the Gospel, which must not be excluded
according to the passage in Peter.

The fact is we need carefully to note the word of our Lord in John
3:8, where He warns us that the Spirit's work in new birth is something
beyond us. We can no more gather it all together in our minds than we
can gather the winds in our fists. The passage in Peter gives us a view of
things from the human side — especially verses 22 and 23 — and the
Armenian seizes them. The passage in John's Epistle views things from
the Divine side, and the Calvinist seizes it. For ourselves, we seize both,
and are not troubled by finding that we can no more mentally adjust the
two sides to perfection than we can adjust and explain the Divine and the
Human in Christ Jesus our Lord, or in the Scriptures of truth.

But is not new birth the very beginning of God's
work in the soul? Are we not absolutely dead,
without the smallest motion Godward, until we are
born again?

We all of us started in a state of absolute spiritual death: there was
no hope for us except God began to work. The story of God's work in
blessing men begins with God and not with man. We are as sure of this as
we are that the story of creation began with God and not with man. God
took the initiative with each of us, and His Spirit began to move on our
hearts just as of old He moved on the face of the waters. But, in the light
of the scriptures we have considered, we can hardly call that first moving

of the Spirit new birth. New birth is a larger and more comprehensive thing, if we take it as presented in Scripture.

And further, new birth is not the antithesis to a state of death, but to a state of corruption. The word which in Scripture stands in antithesis to death is quickening. By new birth we become possessed of a nature which cannot sin, and, hence we have "escaped the *corruption* that is in the world through lust" (2 Peter 1:4).

Are new birth and regeneration — as in Titus 3:5 — the same thing?

They are not. The word translated "regeneration" only occurs twice in Scripture, and both times it has the significance of the new order of things to be brought about in the millennial age. Titus 3:5 however speaks of "the *washing* of regeneration", and we believe that though the regeneration is not the new birth, the "washing" is; and that verse is just Ezekiel 36:25–27 put into New Testament language. Israel will be born again, and thus cleansed from their corruptions in view of the millennial age. We have not had to wait till that age dawns. The washing connected with that coming age reached the heathen Cretians so that they might be cleansed — no longer, "liars, evil beasts, slow bellies" — and therefore should "live soberly, righteously and godly".

That same washing has reached us. We are no longer dominated by corruption, since born of incorruptible seed.

Chapter Eight

———————

QUICKENING

Only when we take a wide view of our fallen estate can we realize in an adequate way the complete havoc that has been wrought by sin, or the fulness of God's answer to it all which reaches us in the Gospel. We have already seen that sin has brought in:

guilt, and so *forgiveness* must reach us;
condemnation, so *justification* is needed;
bondage, and we need *redemption*;
alienation from God, so we need *reconciliation*;
peril of many kinds, so we need *salvation*;
profanation and pollution, so we need *sanctification*;
corruption, which has affected the deepest springs of our nature, so we need the *new birth*.

We have now to see that it has plunged us into spiritual *death*, and we must be *quickened* if we are to live to God.

Our state is set forth in Ephesians 2:1, as "dead in trespasses and sins". The next verse remarkably enough goes on to speak of walking in those trespasses and sins; but that is because the death there spoken of is death *towards God*. Those who are dead Godward are very much alive to "the course of this world", and "the prince of the power of the air", who operates in the "children of disobedience". To be dead towards God is entirely consistent with being alive towards the world and the devil: indeed the one springs out of the other.

This is the fact that underlies the solemn statement made in Romans 3:11, that, "there is none that understandeth, there is none that seeketh after God". That there should be none righteous (verse 10) is bad: it is worse that none should understand, for that means a state not only of ignorance but insensibility. It is worst of all that none should desire to understand or seek after God, with whom is righteousness and understanding and life. To the natural man there is nothing that is desirable in God. Man is not right: he does *not* understand that he is not right: he has *no* desire after God who is right. In one word he is *dead* towards God.

Once these solemn facts lay hold of us, we realize that our only hope is in God taking the initiative with us in His sovereign mercy. We are quite well able to take the initiative in evil, but as regards all that is of God we are dead; and hence all movements must spring from Him.

God then must act. But *how* must He act? Will reformation, education or instruction meet our case? By no means: there can be nothing until He quickens, for quickening simply means the giving of life. The very word translated "quicken" in the New Testament is one compounded of the noun "life", and the verb "to make" — to make to live.

Now it is a striking fact that Ezekiel 36, which shows *the corruption* and moral filth in which Israel lay, and prophesies as to the *new birth* which consequently must be theirs, is followed by the vision of the valley of dry bones in chapter 37. This sets forth the *death* towards God, in which Israel lies as a nation, and it prophesies concerning God's work of *quickening*, which must touch them before they enter into millennial blessedness. They will be brought up by Him out of the graves among the nations where they lie. There will be a national resurrection, and, says the Lord, "Ye shall live, and I shall place you in your own land: then shall ye know that I the Lord have spoken it. and performed it" (verse 14). Once they are quickened they *will understand* and they will at once *seek* the Lord.

The "wind" or "breath", of verse 9 seems to be identified with "My Spirit", of verse 14: indeed, the same Hebrew word is translated, wind, breath or spirit, according to the context. It is interesting to compare these verses with John 3:8. There the blowing of the wind is connected with the Spirit's action in quickening. This should show us how closely new birth and quickening are connected one with the other, and that they must not be divided from each other, though they should be distinguished and separately considered, as they are in chapters 36, and 37, of Ezekiel.

Now if John 3 answers to Ezekiel 36, John 5 answers to Ezekiel 37. That chapter opens with the cure of the impotent man. It was as though a fresh stream of life entered his powerless limbs, and he took up his bed and walked. When challenged as to this miracle, the Lord Jesus proceeded to speak of far greater works than this which were His to do — the quickening of whom He will and the raising of all men. The former is a limited work. Those among the spiritually dead who hear the voice of the Son of God — and only those — shall spiritually live. The latter is universal. All in the graves shall hear His voice and come forth in two classes, to life and to judgment respectively. This will take place at different times, as we learn from other scriptures.

In verse 21 of this marvellous chapter in John, quickening is attributed to both the Father and the Son whereas in the next verse the work of judgment is said to lie wholly in the hands of the Son. The Son, and the Son alone, came forth into this world to suffer and be set at naught. To Him alone then shall the supremacy and majesty and honour of executing judgment belong. In the giving of life however the Son acts according to His own will equally with the Father and — we hardly need add — in fullest accord with the Father. Equally with the Father is He the Source of life, for verse 26 is evidently parallel with verse 21 in its sense. As 1 Corinthians 15: 45 says, "the last Adam . . . a quickening Spirit."

Verses 24 and 25 give us the way in which the Son acts in life-giving power at the present moment. He quickens by means of His word; that is, they hear in it "the voice of the Son of God", and consequently they believe on the Father who sent Him, and they live. Quickening is not presented here as a work of the Son altogether apart from the use of means. Were it so presented we should read, "they that live shall hear". But what we read is, "they that hear shall live". Life is indeed His gift, but it reaches us in the hearing of His voice in His word.

In the light of this chapter we believe we may speak of quickening as the most deep-seated and fundamental aspect of God's work in us. Such is its importance that the Father and the Son act together as to it in a special way. A wrong use is sometimes made of our Lord's statements in verses 19 and 30; "The Son can do nothing of Himself, but what He seeth the Father do"; and "I can of Mine own Self do nothing". These words do not mean that He disclaimed all power, just as a mere prophet might have done. They expressed in the first place the fact that in becoming Man the Son had taken the place of dependent service, acting wholly by the Spirit in subjection to the Father. This thought seems specially prominent in verse 30. But in the second place they also emphasized the fact that His essential place in the unity of the Godhead was such that it was impossible that He should act apart from the Father. This thought seems more prominent in verse 19.

From this inner and more hidden aspect of things it was as though He said, "I am so essentially one with the Father that it is in the nature of things impossible that I should act apart from Him." It was really the strongest possible affirmation of His essential Deity. The Father and the Son must ever act together as the end of verse 19 says. Thus did the Lord *accept* the charge of "making Himself equal with God", and not only accept it but *amplify* the thought of it. So both the Father and the Son act together in life-giving power.

In John 6:63, we discover that the Spirit of God also quickens. The first occurrence of the word "Spirit" in that verse should evidently be printed with a capital, the second occurrence of the word is rightly printed without a capital. Comparison may be made with verse 6 of chapter 3, where the distinction is rightly made. The very words of the Lord are spirit and life but it is the Spirit Himself who quickens. We may say therefore that the whole fulness of the Godhead — Father, Son and Holy Spirit — is involved in the work of giving life to such as ourselves.

One further thing has to be noted. We meet with it both in Ephesians 2:5, and Colossians 2:13 — we have been quickened "together with Christ". Being "dead in trespasses and sins" (Eph. 2:1), and "dead in your sins and the uncircumcision of your flesh" (Col. 2:13), nothing short of quickening would meet our case. Quickening was thus a necessity, but there was no necessity that we should be quickened *together with Christ*: that is the fruit of the counsels of God in grace.

Life "together with", — in association with — Christ was His thought for us, and this goes far beyond the bare necessity of the plight we were in. Life of *some* sort we must have, if ever we were to be in conscious blessedness; but life of *this* sort is the highest and most intimate that can be known by the redeemed creature. Therefore it is that we read of this quickening as being the fruit of the richness of God's mercy, and because of His great love wherewith He loved us. *Rich* mercy and *great* love are thus expressed.

We have been made to live in association with Christ, inasmuch as our life as quickened is of His own order — His life is ours. Since this is so, it is possible for us to be raised up and made to "sit together in heavenly places" in Him. Having life of such an order as this, we are fitted for such exalted seats. The wonderful story of our quickening ends in our sitting in heavenly places in the life of our Quickener.

> In the Old Testament we read of quickening. Ten times or more the Psalmist speaks of it in Psalm 119. Are we to differentiate between that and what we find in the New Testament?

We believe that we have to do so. The Psalmist says that God's word has quickened him in verse 50, yet again and again he desires to be quickened. The word is evidently used more in the sense of being revived, of being restored to more vigorous life. In Old Testament times man was still under probation. The law had been given to test him, and life on earth was still proposed as the result of perfect obedience to the law. Only when we come to the New Testament is the probation period over, and man formally pronounced to be dead in trespasses and sins. Hence only in the New Testament does the full truth of quickening appear.

> Some have thought that quickening is very advanced truth; that, for instance, a man may be born again and yet quickening lie ahead as something to be reached much later, as a kind of climax to God's work in him. Does Scripture indicate this?

It clearly does not. Until quickened by Divine power we are dead. It is the very beginning of God's work in us rather than the climax. It would however be true to say that it is truth into the full import of which we are slow to enter. Almost invariably we begin by understanding truth as to the forgiveness of sins and salvation. This matter of life, and more especially life together with Christ, begins to impress us later in our spiritual history. We must not however attribute to *the thing itself*, what may quite rightly be stated as to our *apprehension* of the thing. The thing itself is the fruit of a Divine act: our apprehension of it the fruit of Divine teaching.

In John 5:26, we read that the Father (1) raises up the dead, and (2) quickens them. Are we right in differentiating between the two things? And, if so, what is the difference?

We believe that there is a distinct difference. In John 11:25, the Lord Jesus says, "I am the resurrection and the life." Resurrection is one thing and life another; though *for us* they are very intimately *connected*. For the unconverted dead they will be *divorced*. They will be raised and their once dead bodies reanimated, though not quickened, since their resurrection will be that of judgment and not of life, as verse 29 shows. Colossians 2:12, 13, also presents resurrection and quickening as quite distinct things. We are quickened already but resurrection in its fulness is before us. When that moment comes our bodies will be instinct with life, in keeping with what has already taken place as to our souls.

We have in Romans 8:11, a word about the quickening of our "mortal bodies". Is that something that takes place in the present, or is it to be in the future?

That is in the future. It is that God "*shall* also quicken your mortal bodies by His Spirit that dwelleth in you". In the previous verse we have, "The Spirit is life because of righteousness". Both statements refer to the indwelling Spirit. He is life to us in an experimental and practical way now. He *will* quicken our mortal bodies presently, whether He does it in resurrection, for the saints who have died, or by the change of which 1 Corinthians 15:51 speaks, for the saints alive when Jesus comes.

Some people however claim that this quickening of our mortal bodies has to do with the healing of disease: that it is what shall be done for us in the present, if only we claim the fulness of the Spirit.

Yes; and in so saying they read into the passage what is not there. There is nothing about disease or healing in the context. It is not our diseased bodies but our mortal bodies that are to be quickened. In our present condition our bodies are liable to death; when quickened they will no longer be subject to death. If the mortal body of the believer really were quickened now, he would be immortal as to his body; that is, *beyond death*, and not merely beyond disease.

So our reply can be twofold. First, there is an "if" in the verse, but it is not, if we claim the fulness of the Spirit, but, if the Spirit dwell in us — which He does, if we really are believers. Second, it is not healing that is in question but the giving of life from a Divine source. When quickened the mortal body is no longer mortal. It is perfectly obvious that this has not yet taken place with any saint living on earth. If Paul's mortal body had been quickened, for instance, the headsman's axe would never have laid him low. He would still be walking amongst us!

The Lord Jesus, as the Last Adam, quickens, according to 1 Corinthians 15:45. We are right, are we not, in connecting this with the present?

Certainly. He stands in contrast to the first Adam in that verse; not merely in being "spirit", in contrast with "soul", but in that He is not merely "living", but the *Life-giver*. Verse 36 of this chapter reminds us that quickening only applies to that which is dead. Now we were dead spiritually, and quickening of a spiritual sort has already reached us from the last Adam. As the Head of a new race, He has already imparted life — His own life — to us who are of His race.

But then this chapter goes on to consider the case of our bodies which are still mortal. We must bear the image of the heavenly Adam even as regards our bodies, and so the great change will reach us at the coming of the Lord. Then "this mortal" will "put on immortality", and this will be the quickening of our mortal bodies, of which Romans 8:11 speaks.

When that is accomplished, and "Death is swallowed up in victory" (verse 54), the work of quickening as regards ourselves will be carried to its final completion. Then the word that we "shall reign in life by One, Jesus Christ" (Rom. 5:17), shall be fulfilled. Not only *in* life, but *reigning* in it, and that *for ever*.

Chapter Nine

THE GIFT
OF THE
HOLY SPIRIT

We have considered many of the direful consequences of sin; there remains one further effect to be emphasized. It has reduced men to a state of powerlessness. Not only are we fallen into bondage to sin, as we saw when considering *redemption*, but we are totally without power to please God or to serve Him. Now one thing is certain: the creature should within its own limits perfectly serve the Creator.

Power we must have; both to deliver us from the paralysis *internal* to ourselves, which sin has produced, and to enable us to go rightly through *external* circumstances, as those who serve the will of God. Power is conferred upon us, and the wonderful thing is that it should be by the indwelling of the Spirit of God. Something much less than this might have sufficed for us, but nothing short of it has been given of God. The risen Christ, about to go on high, said to His disciples, "Ye shall receive power, after that the Holy Ghost is come upon you: and ye shall be witnesses unto Me" (Acts 1:8). This promise was fulfilled ten days later on the day of Pentecost, as Acts 2 records.

In Ezekiel 36 and 37, as we have seen, there are prophecies as to the work of new birth and quickening, which will be wrought in the remnant of Israel in a coming day, preparing them for millennial blessedness. In both chapters there is mention also of the gift of the Holy Spirit — "I will put My Spirit within you, and cause you to walk in My statutes, and ye shall keep My judgments, and do them" (36:27): "And shall put My Spirit in you, and ye shall live" (37:14). As a consequence of this there will be spiritual life in Israel, which will express itself in active obedience to God's will. As God directs, so they will do. Other Old Testament scriptures have similar predictions, notably the end of Joel 2, which Peter quoted on the day of Pentecost, saying that what had just occurred in their midst was a sample of what Joel had foretold. We shall see however that the gift of the Spirit at Pentecost has in it a fulness and permanence hardly contemplated in Old Testament times.

New birth is produced by the Holy Spirit, and in result we have, as John 3:6, indicates, a new nature which is "spirit" in its essential character. That which is produced by the Spirit's action partakes of His own nature. This must of course be distinguished from the Spirit indwelling men already born again, which is what occurred at Pentecost; and it is very necessary to observe that power is connected, not with the new nature produced by the Spirit, but with the Holy Spirit as a Person, actually indwelling the believer's body. This is quite manifest in the passage, Romans 7:7–8:4.

In Romans 7 we are given the experience of one who is born again, for he possesses "the inward man", which delights in the law of God (verse 22). Consequently he approves what is good and earnestly desires it, yet finds himself unable to practise it. It is not until we reach the Deliverer in "Jesus Christ our Lord" (verse 25), and go on to read of "the law [or, control] of the Spirit of life in Christ Jesus", that we find power to overcome "the law [or, control] of sin and death" (8:2), and to fulfill those things which the law so righteously required (8:4). The *power* that delivers is found in Christ, and in His Spirit, who has been given to us.

This passage in Romans shows us the power that delivers us from the internal paralysis that sin induces, and this of course is a prerequisite, if we are to be marked by power in witness to our risen Lord, which is what is contemplated in Acts 1:8, and also in Luke 24:49. It should be a very sobering thought for all of us, that even as saints no power is *vested* in us. All power for us is vested *in the Spirit of God*, who has been given to us.

The eleven men to whom the Lord spoke were Apostles, on whom as a foundation the church has been built. There had been a powerful work of the Spirit in them, and for three years or more they had been under special instruction, such as no men before had ever had. Yet none of these things conferred the necessary power upon them. However eager they may have been to start their great work of witness, they were at a standstill until the Spirit was given. Not one word of witness did they utter until then. But *then*, their mouths were immediately opened, and with what astonishing results!

We must not overlook the fact that on the day of Pentecost the disciples not merely received the Spirit to indwell them, but "they were all *filled* with the Holy Ghost" (Acts 2:4); and when a believer is filled with Him there is no force *active* within, as a check on His power. This filling of the Spirit is not permanent like His indwelling, for Peter was *again* filled with the Spirit in Acts 4:8, and yet *again*, as we find in verse 31 of the same chapter. When the Spirit does thus fill a believer, the flesh in him is judged and quiescent, and His power is irresistible. Stephen illustrates this; for being full of the Holy Ghost, he was "full of faith and power", and his opponents "were not able to resist the wisdom and the spirit by which he spake" (6:8, 10). Unable to resist, they flew to violence, and their stones battered his body to death, thus destroying that "temple" of the Holy Spirit.

Though the history, recorded in Acts, shows that in practice the filling of the Spirit was occasional, even with the Apostles, we must not forget that all Christians are exhorted to be filled with the Spirit, in Ephesians 5:18. It may surprise us to find such a thing put in contrast with being "drunk with wine", but the fact is that when wine is taken in excess it assumes control of the man and carries him outside himself. All that is from beneath and is evil. The Spirit of God however can control, and carry a man outside himself, in a way that is good and divine. The very good is contrasted with the very evil. If *filled* with the Spirit, all that is not Himself and of Him obviously must be excluded.

Now it is in these other things, that fill so much of our thoughts and time and energies, that the hindrances to the realization of power are to be found; and in this connection we have to contemplate not only things positively evil but many things that are trivial and profitless. Hence we get the word, "Grieve not the Holy Spirit of God" (Eph. 4:20). If we grieve Him, we do not lose His indwelling presence, for the verse continues, "whereby ye are sealed unto the day of redemption". We do however lose much of the benefit of His presence. Both spiritual joy and spiritual power are lost until the grieving thing is put away. Some of the things which grieve are mentioned in the verses which precede and which follow. How much the Spirit of God has been grieved by malice, evil-speaking and bitterness amongst saints. The wonder is that His power is manifested at all!

The Apostle Paul was called and saved that he might be a pattern to us. This 1 Timothy 1:16 informs us. So in his life of service and witness we can see how the power of the Spirit wrought.

Romans 15:15 shows the extraordinary *range* of his service. From Jerusalem and round about to Illyricum — the the modern Albania — he fully preached the Gospel. Within about 25 years he had fully evangelized peoples living in territories covering hundreds of thousands of square miles, travelling on foot with the occasional help of a boat on the sea and an animal on the land. A miraculous feat indeed! One only possible for him as energized by the Spirit of God.

1 Corinthians 2:1–5 shows the *simplicity* of his preaching. All merely human adornments were discarded, that the central fact of the Cross of Christ might be the more plainly revealed. What marked his preachings was "demonstration of the Spirit and of power": so that as regards those who received his message, their faith should stand not in "the wisdom of men, but in the power of God".

2 Corinthians 3:1–6, and 4:1–7, show us the *life-giving power* of Paul's new covenant ministry. His converts were "the epistle of Christ", written "with the Spirit of the *living* God", and, says he, "the Spirit giveth *life*". Both life and light are connected in this passage, for he says, "the light of the knowledge of the glory of God in the face of Jesus Christ" shines through "earthen vessels, that the excellency of the power may be of God, and not of us".

2 Corinthians 10:1–6 shows us the power of *spiritual weapons* in the aggressive conflicts of the Gospel. Satanic powers have entrenched themselves in human minds and formed strongholds of human reasonings and lofty thoughts, which can only be overthrown by such weapons as are employed by the Spirit of God.

1 Thessalonians 1 and 2 give us a lovely picture of the *spiritual fruits* in the characters and lives of the converts, when the Gospel comes "not . . . in word only, but also in power, and in the Holy Ghost, and in much assurance". The Thessalonian believers became *followers* of the Lord, *ensamples* to all other believers, and *propagators* of the Word that

had saved them; as they served the living and true God and waited for His Son from heaven.

2 Timothy 1 shows us the Holy Spirit as characterized by "the spirit . . . of power, and of love, and of a sound mind" (7); so that the believer is enabled to be a "partaker of the afflictions of the Gospel according to the power of God" (8), and also to "keep by the Holy Ghost which dwelleth in us" the good deposit with which he has been entrusted (14). The Spirit of God is the power of *endurance* and for *fidelity*.

The gift of the Spirit on God's part, as well as the gift of His Son, may well be spoken of as "unspeakable" (2 Cor. 9:15).

> At the outset the power of the Spirit was very largely displayed in signs and wonders. Seeing that He is God and unchangeable, should it not be so today?

God is indeed the unchangeable One, but this does not mean that He cannot vary His ways and dealings according to His wisdom, as He meets the changing situations that arise amongst men. He has most evidently done so in past dispensations. The display of His power in miracles has never been constant, indeed only in *three* great epochs has it been manifested thus. First, when through Moses He intervened to bring Israel out of Egypt and into Palestine, inaugurating the law system. Second, when He intervened through Elijah and Elisha, recalling the people to the broken law, and testifying of His goodness. Third, when He intervened in Christ, and the church was subsequently formed through the Apostles. Practically all the miracles that Scripture records come into these three periods. Of John the Baptist we read, "John did no miracle" (John 10:41). His lot was cast just before the third great miracle epoch began in connection with Christ.

> But are not these miraculous signs the very greatest display of His power?

By no means. Most of these visible displays of miraculous energy were only *temporal* in their effects. In Acts 9, for instance, Aeneas was raised up from his sick bed, and Dorcas from her bed of death; but in both cases the passage of years brought them into death, and the miracles were as though they had never been. That chapter opens with the conversion of Saul of Tarsus. His fellow-travellers were speechless with amazement, yet they do not seem to have discerned the miracle. It was of course a spiritual miracle of the first order, the effect of which is felt all over the earth today — just nineteen centuries later. Every true conversion is a miracle which abides *to eternity*; and miracles of this sort are taking place today.

> Paul's preaching was in demonstration of the Spirit
> and of power. Can we speak of modern preaching
> in this way?

Only in a very minor degree, we fear. The fact is that so much modern preaching is marked by the very things which Paul tells us he avoided, in order that his preaching might be in the power of the Spirit. He not only renounced the things of deceit and evil, as he tells us in 2 Corinthians 4:2, but also things of a very reputable sort, such as excellency of speech, and wisdom according to man.

> But even where the Gospel is faithfully preached,
> and that without reliance upon these human
> expedients, there does not seem to be much power
> manifested. How can we explain that?

There are two scriptures which may help to explain it — Ephesians 4:30, and 1 Thessalonians 5:19. All too often the Spirit is grieved in the servant of God who labours, and hence there is little fruit in what he does. And even when this is not the case, the Spirit is grieved by the state of things that prevails amongst the mass of professing Christians. There is also a quenching of the Spirit by the introduction of much human organization, which gives no place to His free action. Then beyond this there is the terrible incubus of unbelief, and often utter infidelity, on the part of multitudes of professed servants of God, who deny practically everything they are pledged to uphold. The Spirit is *grieved* and *quenched* in the bosom of the church, and this fact alone would account for His withholding any great manifestation of His power.

However, it is happily a fact that He is still working, and souls are being blessed, though His work is proceeding in quieter and less noticed ways.

Power for service, though important, is by no means everything. How may we know the Spirit's power for victory in our lives?

By walking in the Spirit, as Galatians 5:16 bids us. We learn from Ephesians 1:13, that He is given to us when we believe the Gospel of our salvation. He marks us off as belonging to God. But also we are to *walk* in Him; that is, He is to be in a practical way the Source and Energy of our life and activities. Walking is the first and earliest activity of mankind, hence it becomes a figurative expression for our activities. Our thoughts, speech and actions are to be under the Spirit's control. Then we shall not be fulfilling the desires of the flesh, as otherwise we should. This is what verse 17 of Galatians 5 says. The Spirit of God wields a power that is superior to the downward drag of the flesh: and we experience it, if we walk in Him.

Some of us would say, that though we desire to "walk in the Spirit", we hardly know how to set about it. How does it work out practically?

Galatians 6:7–9, may help to answer this. Our lives in a practical way are made up of sowing and reaping. It is as though we go forth each day with a seed basket on either side of us. We may put our hand into the basket of the flesh on that side and sow to the flesh, or into the basket of the Spirit on this side and sow to the Spirit: that is, we may be yielding to the things which merely gratify the flesh, and so scatter the seeds of the flesh, or we may give ourselves to the things of the Spirit, and sow seeds that will be fruitful to His glory.

This is not something that God does for us, but what we do ourselves. All day long we are doing it in one or other of these two directions. In which direction does our choice lie? Into which basket are we continually placing our hand? The resolute *refusal* of the one, and the *cultivation* of the other, is the secret. That is the way to set about it.

> Still, many a Christian who is not guilty of serious lapses in outward conduct, is not particularly marked by the liberty or power of the Spirit. How is that to be accounted for?

Such are probably marked by lack of concentration upon the things of God, or by positive laziness. They are easily diverted to things of trifling worth. The Spirit is here to take of the things of Christ and show them unto us, and He may be grieved by *inattention* or *sloth* on our side. If you went to an acquaintance with important tidings from a much loved friend, and in a few moments he were to interrupt your glowing story with irrelevant remarks about trivialities, or you found him inclined to sleep in his chair, you would cease your story, grieved and indignant.

The Spirit of God is sensitive as to that which concerns the glory of Christ. Inattention will grieve Him as well as open sin. Let us each ask God to show us how much of our spiritual poverty and powerlessness is to be traced to this.

Chapter Ten

NEW CREATION

As we have considered in detail most of the features that go to make up the "great salvation" which has reached us, we have hitherto been able to point out how each is designed of God to meet and overcome some particular result or penalty of sin. But now in this chapter, this feature has to be absent. We have left "new creation" until now as it seems to be the ultimate thing to which the Gospel conducts us, but at the same time it is evident that God is going to establish it, not because it meets some definite need *on our side*, but because it meets the need of His holy nature — it is the thing which is suitable *to Himself*.

The havoc wrought by sin has been such that we *needed* forgiveness, justification, reconciliation, redemption, salvation, sanctification; and all these are brought to us in the Gospel as the fruit of the work done for us by our Lord Jesus Christ on the Cross. Equally did we *need* the new birth, the quickening, the gift of the Spirit; and the first two of these are ours by the work of the Holy Spirit in us, while His indwelling follows the other two, and is based upon the work done for us. We could hardly say however in the same way that we *needed* to be newly "created in Christ Jesus"; that wondrous event has taken place to satisfy the heart of God.

As in other cases so again here, we can go back to the Old Testament and discover prophecies which foreshadow the full truth, which can only be discovered in the New. For instance, we read, "Behold, I create new heavens and a new earth" (Isaiah 65:17): yet when we examine the context we soon see that what is predicted in Revelation 21:1–5, is hardly contemplated in the passage, for the prophet goes on to speak of the new conditions that will prevail in Jerusalem in the millennial age, when death may possibly take place; whereas in the scene pictured in Revelation death is gone for ever.

The fact seems to be, that just as with new birth and quickening, so again here, God introduces His thought; but in a limited way as befitted a dispensation in which His government of the earth was the prominent thing. In this Gospel age, life and incorruptibility have been fully brought to light, and in connection with that His full thought and action, both as regards the work of Christ for us and the work of the Spirit in us, has been manifested. The New Testament does not stop at the millennial age but carries us into the eternal state.

The first mention of new creation in the New Testament is in 2 Corinthians 5:17, where we find that every one "in Christ" is brought into it. It is "new creation" in this verse rather than "a new creature", and the language of Paul here appears to be very vigorous and emphatic. He omits the verb altogether, and exclaims, "So that, if anyone in Christ — new creation!" as one who exults in this glorious fact. Nothing short of this is involved in our being in Christ Jesus.

That the believer is in Christ Jesus and beyond all condemnation is made very plain in the Epistle to the Romans, but we are not carried on to the full implication of that fact until we reach this scripture. We are *in* Him because we are *of* Him, and this by an act of God Himself. This comes very definitely to view when we reach Ephesians 2:10, "We are His workmanship, created in Christ Jesus." The old creation of which we read in Genesis 1, was God's workmanship and created by the Son. It was created by Him, but not created *in* Him, as the new creation is, at least as regards ourselves. Sin was able to gain an entrance into the old creation, but it will never enter the new, which derives its life and nature from Christ.

The passage in 2 Corinthians 5 shows that there is a very close connection between reconciliation and new creation. The former is one of the fruits of the work of Christ for us; the latter the fruit of God's work in us. Yet of course the act of God in making "Him to be sin for us, who knew no sin", with which the chapter closes, is the basis on which rests new creation no less than reconciliation. There must be the complete meeting of every liability and the whole state characterizing the old creation, if the new creation is to be introduced on a righteous basis.

There is no patching up of the old things in connection with new creation. They pass away, and new things which are wholly "of God" are introduced. Once even Christ Himself stooped into old creation circumstances, when He was amongst us "after the flesh", though His flesh was holy and without the least taint of sin. Now, in His risen glory, he has entered into new creation circumstances, and from Him as Head the new creation proceeds.

The main point in this passage however seems to be the subjective effect of new creation in ourselves. We know Christ in a new way, all things are become new to us, our lives are diverted into a totally new channel, so that we live not unto ourselves but unto Him — all this, because of God's new creation work wrought in us. As an illustration we might take the Apostles, as they *were* in the Gospels and as they *became* in the Acts. Between the two came the new creation in-breathing of the Last Adam, of John 20:22, and the indwelling of the Spirit, of Acts 2. Formerly they knew Him after the flesh; now their knowledge of Him is according to the Spirit of God. There was undoubtedly a change in *His* condition, but we must not overlook the great change in *their* condition.

This side of things is emphasized by the fact that we are said to "know . . . *no man* after the flesh". Now with the great mass of men there is no change at all in *their* condition, the only change is *in ourselves*. It is because we are a new creation in Christ that we know everyone in a new way. We look upon all men and everything with new creation eyes — if we may so put it.

What we have just been looking at is the new creation *mind* found in the saints; whereas Ephesians 2:10 brings us to new creation *practice* and *action*. We are created "unto good works", in which God purposes we should walk. James, in his second chapter, speaks not of good works but of the works of faith; that is of work energized by *faith*, and consequently manifesting *it* before the eyes of men. Here we do have *good* works; that is, works that express the goodness of God. Being God's workmanship, created by Him in Christ Jesus, we have the inward capacity to do works of this exalted character, and the obligation to do them rests upon us. These good works were supremely and perfectly done by Christ, and as created in Christ, we are to walk in them —

works of that order, though of course not in the same measure as He.

What we find in Ephesians 4:21–24, and in Colossians 3:10, is in keeping with this. The former passage agrees with the latter, for the New Translation renders it, "Your *having* put off . . . and *being* renewed . . . and your *having* put on"; that is, in both passages the great transaction is viewed as one *accomplished* in every believer. Formerly we belonged to the old order of man and wore his corrupt character: now we belong to the new order of man and wear his character, marked by holiness, righteousness, truth. It is not something merely external, for the very *spirit* of our *minds* is renewed. The passage in Colossians corroborates this, though it has distinctive differences. It also speaks of the new man as *created*.

It is because we have put on this new creation character that we are to behave as indicated in the context of both passages. The things to be utterly repudiated, and the things to be cultivated, are all determined by the character we wear by God's new creation act.

We may go one step further, and in the light of Ephesians 2:15, speak of the church as God's new creation production. By the Gospel, God is calling an election out of both Jew and Gentile, and of the two He is making "one new man". The word translated in that verse "make" is the word for "create". That one new man is God's creation by the Lord Jesus, for He is the Actor in that verse. And He creates this one new man, which is virtually the church, "in Himself". So we may speak of the church, as well as the individual saint, as a new creation in Christ Jesus.

Lastly, in Revelation 21:1–6, we are permitted to know that there are to be new heavens and a new earth, and amidst these new creation scenes the new creation church will have her eternal home, as the tabernacle of God, when He dwells with men.

Are we right, in dealing with the new creation, if we give the same literal and full meaning to the word "create", that we give to it when dealing with the creation of Genesis 1?

We believe that we are. Any difficulty that is felt about it probably springs from the fact that as yet God's new creation work has not touched any of the material things round about us. It has so far only affected *us* spiritually: we are renewed in the *spirit* of our minds. It is quite certain we are not yet newly created as to our bodies, and that probably accounts for the scripture saying, "renewed in the spirit of your mind"; for the mind cannot be altogether dissociated from the brain, which is a part of the body. When we are in our glorified bodies, in the likeness of Christ, and dwelling in the new heavens and new earth, we shall see that no word short of "creation" will meet the case. But what we are today in a spiritual way, as the fruit of God's workmanship, is exactly of that order. God says it, and we may happily believe it.

The fact that we have been created "in Christ Jesus" has been mentioned. Are we to deduce from this the stability of the new creation?

We certainly are: but more than that also, we believe. Since it is created in Him, it will be as stable as He is; but also it will bear His character in other things. It originates in Him, for He is the Source whence it springs. He is "the beginning, the Firstborn from the dead" (Col. 1: 18), "the Beginning of the creation of God" (Rev. 3:14). Even the inanimate things of the new heavens and the new earth will spring from Him, yet we are created in Him in a deeper sense. He has entered heaven in His risen Manhood, and we now are men of His order, participating in His life, "all of one" with Him, as we are told in Hebrews 2:11. Hence the church is His body, for in it corporately He is to be expressed. The new creation will be expressive of Christ and as stable as He.

In Hebrews 8:13, it is pointed out that the fact of a new covenant being introduced makes the first covenant old; and the deduction is, "Now that which decayeth and waxeth old is ready to vanish away." Can we reason in the same way in regard to the new creation?

We believe so; with this modification perhaps, that not all the heavens created in Genesis 1, have been touched by sin, consequently not all will be newly created. All that has been spoiled by sin is old and ready to vanish away. Nothing less than new creation will meet the case, just as nothing short of it meets our spiritual needs today, because all has to be lifted to the level of the Divine thoughts. In principle it is so today, as we see in Galatians 6:15. The Galatians were being diverted to the ordinance of circumcision as practised under the law. But any such ordinance or other fleshly observance is entirely beside the mark today. It might be all right so long as men "in Adam" were recognized as having a standing before God; but "in Christ Jesus" neither circumcision nor uncircumcision is of any account; a new creation alone avails. Because of what God is, once a thing has been touched and tarnished by sin, it has to go and a new creation take its place.

Are the new creation scenes predicted in the opening part of Revelation 21, to be distinguished from the scenes of millennial blessedness, of which the prophets have so largely spoken?

The two scenes are clearly distinguished in that chapter in Revelation. Verses 1–8, deal with the eternal state, whilst verses 9–27, gives us a more detailed description of the heavenly Jerusalem in its relations with the millennial earth. Hence in the second section we read about nations and kings of the earth, and walls and gates which shut out any defiling thing. This supposes of course that there are defiling things which might enter. In the earlier part all sin and sorrow and death are gone from God's fair new creation, and all evil lies under God's judgment, segregated in its own appointed place.

Nations, too, only exist as the result of God's judgment upon men at Babel; so they disappear, and God will revert to His original thought and just dwell with men. He will dwell as their God in holy freedom because righteousness will then be dwelling, as 2 Peter 3:13 tells us, and not merely reigning, as it will in the millennial age. As long as there is anything to challenge its supremacy it must reign: when the last challenge is met, it will dwell in undisturbed repose.

Will all differences between men disappear in the new creation?

It may be that on the new earth they will: as to that we cannot dogmatize. But at all events there will be the difference between those whose seat is to be in the heavens and those on the earth. In that day the holy city, symbolic of the church, will be the dwelling-place of God.

Again, in 1 Corinthians 15, where we find that already we have been quickened by the Last Adam, we also learn that His great work with us will reach its completion when we "bear the image of the Heavenly". It is a most marvellous fact that we, who belong to the church, shall enter those new creation scenes bearing the image of our Head even as regards our bodies. We do not find this asserted of others, besides the heavenly saints.

It is quickening which is actually mentioned in 1 Corinthians 15, though we have referred to it in connection with new creation. This rather raises the question as to what is the relationship between the two things; and indeed between all the things we have considered. How can we put them all together?

There are things connected with our most holy faith which are quite beyond our powers, and this is one of them. We contemplate our Lord Jesus, we confess His Deity, whilst recognizing His true Humanity, yet our minds are not equal to the task of explaining how both go together. We see the sovereignty of God plainly taught in Scripture, and the responsibility of man taught with equal plainness, yet how exactly to adjust them together we know not. This inability of ours does not disturb us. We expect it, because the faith, which we believe, comes from God. Could we bring it all within the compass of our little minds we should thereby prove it was not Divine.

Now how can we put together all the things we have been surveying in cursory fashion? We may do so in part, but we cannot do so in any complete way, especially when we deal with the work wrought in us. The attempt to do so in the past has often led to unprofitable contentions, as might be expected. We repeat that we can no more see all round the subject at the same moment than we can see all four sides of a house at once.

The truth is one; of that we are sure. It is given to us in parts; and as we trace out these parts in Scripture we are instructed and profited. If we fail to distinguish things that differ, and lump them all together in a kind of indiscriminate mass, we lose a great deal. On the other hand if we divorce and divide the various parts we soon run into erroneous notions, as also we do if we attempt to work out theories as to the order in which they take place.

Without dividing we distinguish, and thereby understand more fully how rich and varied is the great salvation which has reached us. And the more we do understand, the more our hearts are moved in praise and thanksgiving to God.

Chapter Eleven

FAITH AND WORKS

It has been commonly supposed that between faith and works a deadly feud exists; so much so that they are utterly irreconcilable. This is far from being true. Most mistaken ideas have, however, a grain of truth embedded in them somewhere, and this one is no exception to the rule. It is perfectly true that the popular doctrine of salvation by human merit, in the shape of works of some kind or other, is totally opposed to and inconsistent with the Bible truth of justification by faith. Yet the Scriptures speak of good works, but they are of another order altogether and are as much in harmony with faith, and as intimately connected with it as the fruit and leaves of a tree with the sap which flows through trunk and branches.

If we open our Bibles at Colossians 1:21, we find the expression "*wicked works.*" These there is no need to define. They are the hideous outcome of the fallen and depraved nature of the children of Adam. The bad fruit of a bad tree.

In Hebrews 9:14, we get the words "*dead works.*" These are works done with the object of obtaining life and blessing, such as the diligent performance of religious duties and observances. They are man's "righteousnesses," which are only as "filthy rags" in God's sight (Isaiah 64:6) — the product of the bad tree when cultivated to the utmost. Bad fruit after all, for no amount of skill can produce grapes from thorns, or figs from thistles.

In Titus 2:7,9 we have "*good works*" spoken of, and strongly enforced upon Christians. They are the fruit of that new life and nature of which the Christian partakes, which has its vitality in faith, and of which the Spirit of God is the power. They are the good fruit which grows upon the good tree.

In the Epistle to the Romans, chapters 3, 4, and 5, justification before God is seen to be solely on the principle of faith. One verse will be sufficient proof.

"Therefore we conclude that a man is justified *by faith without the deeds of the law*" (3:28).

In the second chapter of James we have it laid down with equal clearness that justification — as a public thing in this world before men — is not only or mainly by faith, but by works. One verse again will suffice to prove it.

"Ye see, then, how that by *works* a man is justified, *and not by faith only*" (verse 24).

Study carefully the context of these two passages, and you will see a most striking proof of the harmony that exists between faith and works. Both Paul in Romans and James in his Epistle cite Abraham as the great Old Testament example which supports their contention. In the life of that remarkable man called out of God to become "the father of all them that *believe*" (Rom. 4:11), we see *faith* as a living reality between his soul and God; when gazing into the starlit heavens he "believed God" — accepting as certain that which was humanly impossible — "and it was counted unto him for righteousness." We also see a great *work* of faith when years afterwards, in simple obedience, he went forth to Mount Moriah to sacrifice Isaac, in whom the promises reposed. He believed in God as a God who raises the dead. This public act proved it beyond dispute before men. It was the outward evidence of the inward faith.

The former we find in Genesis 15, and to this Paul appeals in Romans 4. The latter is recorded in Genesis 22, and to it James refers.

Like the fable which tells of two men, one inside a hollow ball, the other outside — one declaring it to be concave, the other insisting upon its being convex — Paul gives us the inside view, and cries "by faith." James viewing things externally, says "by works" — only, unlike the fable, in so saying, they do not disagree over it.

But now for some questions.

What is Faith?

Elaborate definitions might be given, but they would probably be less satisfactory than the answer made by a little child to this very question. She simply replied, "Believing what God says, *because God says it.*"

Faith is like a window. It receives the light. The sunlight is there. It shines *upon* the wall outside, but *in* at the window; nothing is added to it, but its rays illumine the otherwise darkened room. To "believe God" like Abraham lets Divine light come streaming into the soul.

But faith is more than this. It means not only to have light, but to *wholly repose on the One whom the light reveals to us.*

The late Dr. Paton of the New Hebrides used to tell that when translating the Scriptures into the tongue of the islanders he failed for some time to find an appropriate word for "trusting" or "believing."

One day, however, he called an intelligent Christian native, and seating himself on a chair he said, "What am I doing?"

"Master, you are resting," said the woman.

The doctor had heard that word before; it was not what he wanted, but a bright idea struck him.

He lifted both feet off the ground, and placing them under him so that they rested on the rail between the front legs of the chair, he said, "Now what am I doing?"

"Oh, master!" said the woman, "you are resting wholly, you are trusting," using a word quite new to the doctor's ears. That was the word he wanted!

Faith is reposing wholly upon Christ — *with both feet off the ground.*

What are we to understand by that verse which says that a believer's faith is counted for righteousness? (Rom. 4:5).

We must not read those words with a *commercial* idea in our minds, as though they meant that we come to God bringing so much faith for which we receive in exchange so much righteousness, just as a shopkeeper across his counter exchanges goods for cash.

Nor must we entertain a *chemical* idea, as though they meant that we bring our faith that it may be transmuted into righteousness, after the fashion of the fabled philosopher's stone that turns everything it touches into gold!

No! Abraham is the great example of what is meant (verse 3). He — and we — are accounted or held by God as righteous in view of faith. That is its simple meaning. Faith brings in all the justifying merits of the blood of Christ; these are the great basis of that righteousness; and further, it may safely be said that the first right (or righteous) thing in anybody's life, and the beginning of a course which is right, is when he turns to God as a sinner, and believes on the Lord Jesus Christ.

There are verses which seem to connect works with salvation. Philippians 2:12, for instance. How should we understand them?

Always strictly in relation to their context. Even if we had no context to refer to, we might be sure that "work out your own salvation" is not intended to clash with the truth of Ephesians 2:8,9, "For by grace are ye saved through faith . . . not of works lest any man should boast."

Turning, however, to the context we find that the Apostle's subject in Philippians 1 and 2 is the practical walk of the believer. Adversaries were abounding (1:28). Difficulties were thickening in the bosom of the Church (2:2–4). Paul himself, the watchful pastor, was removed far from them (2:12). In effect, he says, "Christ Jesus is your great Example. With fear and trembling, because conscious of your weakness with the flesh within, work out your own salvation from the various forms of evil which threaten you." And lest they should think of their own abilities for one moment he adds, *"for it is God which worketh in you."* By His Spirit He works *in* and we work *out*.

Might not the preaching of "only believe" without demanding good works lead to disastrous results?

Yes. To preach "only believe" in an indiscriminate way may lead to mischief. We shall not improve upon apostolic methods, so let us see what Paul did.

To men generally he testified, "*Repentance* toward God, and faith toward our Lord Jesus Christ" (Acts 20:21).

When speaking to the anxious jailer of Philippi, in whose soul a work of repentance was already proceeding, he said *only*, "Believe on the Lord Jesus Christ, and thou shalt be saved" (Acts 16:31). There "only believe" was quite in place, and to have "demanded good works" would have been worse than vain. It is recorded, however, that within one short hour of conversion the jailer performed his first good work, the fruit and proof of his faith (*see* verse 33). He did it not in order to be saved, but as the result of the change that grace had wrought within.

Paul further tells us that he preached that men should "repent, and turn to God, and do works meet for repentance" (Acts 26:20). This is most needful. If a man professes repentance we may safely demand that the change shall become manifest in his daily life ere we fully accept his professions. But this has nothing to do with preaching good works as an auxiliary to our justification.

Not only have we "dead works" in Hebrews, but "dead faith" in James 2:17. What is this latter?

It is human faith, mere head belief, and not the living faith that finds its spring in God. Demons share this faith, as the succeeding verses show. It appears superficially to be much like real faith, but on closer inspection it is seen to be spurious. It "hath not works." It is a fruitless tree, with nothing but leaves.

Scripture furnishes us with examples of this dead faith. Read John 2:23–25 and compare therewith 6:66–71. In that scene, living faith is exemplified by Simon Peter; dead faith by the many disciples who left Jesus, whilst Judas Iscariot gives us a man with much profession and no faith at all!

Many professing Christians have little or nothing to show in the way of good works. What does it mean?

Who can really tell but God alone? Good works are not so much like the works inside the watch as the hands upon its face, which indicate the result of the activity within. Faith is the mainspring of the activity. It may be that such people are *only* professors, like a toy watch with hands only painted on its face, and no insides at all! Or it may be that something has gone wrong with the works within; they are true Christians, but sunk into a low and carnal condition like the man of whom Peter speaks, who is "blind and cannot see afar off, and hath forgotten that he was purged from his old sins" (2 Peter 1:9).

At any rate, the principle holds good that "the tree is known by his fruit" (Matt. 12:33). Remembering also that "the Christian is the world's Bible," we can well understand the stress laid on the importance of good works in Scripture (*see* Ephesians 2:10; 1 Peter 2:9–12; and the whole of Titus 2).

How will the believer's works on earth affect his place in heaven?

Not at all. A place in heaven is his solely on the ground of the work of Christ. The Father "hath made us meet to be partakers of the inheritance of the saints in light" (Col. 1:12). With that our works have nothing to do. All is of grace. There is only one title to a place in heaven, and that *every* true Christian has.

Our works will, however, greatly affect our place in the kingdom of our Lord Jesus Christ, as shown in the well-known parables of the "talents" (Matt. 25) and the "pounds" (Luke 19). The same thing is clearly taught in 2 Peter 1:5–11, where, after urging the Christians to whom he wrote to abound in every spiritual grace and work, he says, "For *so* an entrance shall be ministered unto you *abundantly* into" — heaven? No. "The everlasting kingdom of our Lord and Saviour Jesus Christ."

The *character* of our entrance into that does depend upon our works.

Chapter Twelve

———————

PEACE AND DELIVERANCE

Let us begin by comparing two scriptures which will bring our subject fairly before us. The first is Romans 5:1. "Therefore being justified by faith, we have peace with God through our Lord Jesus Christ."

The second, Romans 7:24,25.

"O wretched man that I am! who shall deliver me from this body of death? [*margin*]. I thank God through Jesus Christ our Lord."

Peace with God, and deliverance from sin and the flesh within, are two great blessings, which the Gospel of God brings to us all. They go hand in hand, yet they are distinct. It is well for us to understand the difference between them, as also the way in which each is made our own. The cross of Christ of course is the great basis of both.

We may notice in the first place that the mischievous results of sin are seen in two directions, *externally* and *internally*.

Externally sin has severed the once happy link that united man, as an intelligent creature, to his Creator. Satan succeeded at the outset in using it to cut the line of communication between man and his true base of operations — God Himself, and ever since the human race has been in the position of the little city of which Solomon speaks. The great king has come against it, besieged it, and built great bulwarks against it (Eccles.9:14).

Sin has thus brought in distance, estrangement, and enmity on man's side against God, and all his relations Godward are in the direst confusion.

Internally, the wreck is no less complete. The sources of life have been poisoned; the mainspring of man's will and affection has broken. Chaos reigns supreme in the mind and heart of every sinner. Instead of his being joyous and free, moving with intelligent subjection in the sunlight of God's favour, he is in bondage. Instead of being master of himself, sin is his master. Instead of his spirit being in control of mind and body, it has become like a captain of a vessel, overpowered and battened down beneath hatches, at the mercy of a whole crew of evil passions and lusts.

Some years ago the eyes of Europe, and indeed of the world, were specially drawn towards Russia. No nation presented just then a more pitiable spectacle. She was involved *externally* in a disastrous war, and *internally* in ruinous conflict, upheavals, and anarchy, until it looked as if her very existence as a nation was threatened. Her state at that time not inaptly illustrates our present theme.

Read Romans, chapters 1 to 3, and you will find the awful state portrayed, into which sin has plunged man as regards his relations with God. Then the divine remedy in the death and resurrection of Christ is set forth, and the result of this is *for faith*, "peace with God."

Then read chapter 7. What a revelation of internal anarchy and confusion! Into what a tangle of conflicting desires, emotions, and struggles has not sin plunged us! But out of all this we may emerge, thanks to the cross of Christ and the Spirit's power (8:1–4), and the result here is "deliverance from the body of this death."

Peace, then, is "with God," the result of having all our relations with Him placed on a righteous and satisfactory footing through the work of Christ.

Deliverance is "from this body of death," *i.e.*, from this putrid corpse of corruption, which we each of us carry about within ourselves, the result of sin in the flesh.

There is, then, a clear distinction between these two great blessings, and yet both are declared to be "through Jesus Christ our Lord." His cross is the basis of both. It was at one and the same time the complete answer to all our guilt, so that we who believe are justified by God Himself (3:25,26), and also the full condemnation of all that we were in ourselves as self-destroyed children of Adam (6:6; 8:3), so that deliverance might reach us in the power of the risen Christ.

But though the basis of both is evidently the same, there is a difference between the ways in which they are received by us.

Peace, though it is preceded always by the anxiety, which is produced by having the eyes opened to one's dangerous position in regard to God, is distinctly said to be by *faith* (Rom. 5:1). Many of us remember — do we not? — when out of the anxious depths our eyes were suddenly opened to gaze in faith on the once crucified, but now risen, Saviour. We saw every question settled, every obstacle removed, every cloud once between us and God rolled away; we could truthfully sing:

"From sinking sand He lifted me;
With tender hand He lifted me;
From shades of night to plains of light,
Oh, praise His Name, He lifted me!"

In one word the result was — "Peace."

Deliverance, on the other hand, though it cannot be apart from faith, is largely linked up with *experience*. We wade through the mire of Romans 7 to reach the rock which rises before us at the end of the chapter. We learn useful, but painful, lessons of "no good in the flesh" (5:18), "no power in our best desires" (verse 23), even when those desires are the result of a new nature within, called here "the law of my mind," "the inward man." Then it is that, heartsick of sin and self, the weary soul looks for an outside deliverer, and finds one in the Lord Jesus Christ.

That deliverance is found in the knowledge of the meaning of Christ's cross as the condemnation of sin in the flesh, and in the power of the Spirit of God, who makes Christ so truly "a living bright Reality," that under His warm influence order begins to appear out of chaos, and victory is obtained over sin.

Is it possible to have one's sins forgiven and yet not have peace?

Upon what, then, does forgiveness depend? Evidently upon simple *faith in Christ*. "Whosoever believeth in Him shall receive remission of sins" is what Scripture says (Acts 10:43).

Upon what does peace depend? Upon *faith in the Gospel of God*, which sets before us a Saviour "who was delivered for our offences, and was raised again for our justification" (Rom. 4:25).

The question then resolves itself into: "Is it possible to simply believe in Christ, and wholly trust in Him as a poor sinner, without believing with equal simplicity the Gospel message, which sets before us not only Himself, but His work and its results?"

The answer must be, Alas! yes. All too many pay as much, if not more, attention to their feelings than to the unchanging Gospel, and therefore have not peace, though they fully trust in Christ.

Although this is so, such a state of things is not what God intends, nor what Scripture contemplates. It is the fruit of defective teaching, or the product of unbelief.

Must peace and deliverance always be received together? or may they be possessed at different times?

No rule is laid down in Scripture, though they are evidently treated in quite distinct fashion in the Epistle to the Romans. "Peace" is dealt with fully, chapters 1 to 5, before "deliverance" is dealt with, chapters 6 to 8.

In the actual history of Christians, it would seem that most frequently the question of sins, and how to meet God, entirely fills the vision till peace is known, and *afterwards* the Spirit of God raises the question of sin, and the flesh, and victory over both.

Yet there are not a few who would testify that in their cases both questions were involved in their anxieties and exercises, and it seemed as if light on both dawned together. The writer would testify that in his case he never had settled peace until light began to break on the subject of deliverance.

Can it be possible for a person to be continually overcome by sin, as detailed in Romans 7, and yet have peace with God?

Not exactly. Taking the chapter as it stands, one cannot but be struck with what the speaker does *not* mention. In all the verses from 7 to 24, not one allusion does he make to the redemption work of Christ, not one word is uttered as to the Spirit of God. These painful exercises are evidently those of one who, though "born again," and therefore with a new nature, is in his conscience under the law, does not know redemption, and has not the gift of the indwelling Spirit. Hence he is "carnal," "sold under sin," and absolutely *nothing* is right.

Yet the believer, having peace with God, may have an experience of this order, but modified, since he does know redemption and possess the Spirit. Though not sold under sin, and he may be nearly always in the gloom of ignominious failure, though not without one single ray of light, as is pictured in the chapter.

If a really converted person gets such an experience, must it not show that something is radically wrong?

Yes, indeed, but wrong with him, not with his Christianity. The pity is that so many do *not* seem to have the experience. There is something wrong with them, but they don't seem to feel it.

The fact is, to "get into Romans 7" — as some Christians term it — is a sign of spiritual progress rather than the reverse. It betokens a sensitive conscience, and a real desire to walk in the paths of holiness, and the lessons which are learnt during the experience, though painful, are salutary.

Just as no one gets peace without previously being in the throes of soul-anxiety, so no believer reaches that deliverance from sin and self, which issues in a robust type of Christianity, without such an experience as detailed in Romans 7.

What is the secret of getting this deliverance?

Simply looking away from self to Christ. Note the incessant repetition of "I" and "me" — particularly the former — in verses 7 to 24, and then in this last verse the sudden change. Sickened and hopeless, the speaker lifts his eyes off himself and seeks an outside deliverer. It is not, "How shall I deliver myself?" but "Who shall deliver me?"

Is deliverance a thing which, like peace, we get at a definite moment, and once for all?

No. Peace is the result of receiving God's testimony as to the finished work of Christ, and often comes like the lightning's flash. Deliverance, on the other hand, not only depends on the work of Christ for us, but on the work of the Spirit in us. That is not something completed in a moment once for all, but a gradual work, which has not only to be maintained, but increased.

There is, of course, a definite moment when the soul cries out, "O wretched man that I am! who shall deliver me?", a moment when it begins to dawn upon us what it means to be "in Christ Jesus" (8:1), and we first taste the sweetness of the liberty which is the result of coming under the control of "the Spirit of life in Christ Jesus" (verse 2). That is the moment when deliverance begins, but it has to be maintained, and its measure should be increased so long as we are in this world.

Some believers have spent long years in vain struggles against the power of indwelling sin. What would you advise them to do?

Give it up; and look away to the great Deliverer! Lose yourself in the warm beams of His love and glory — that is deliverance indeed.

A well-known minister of the Gospel uses an allegory which aptly illustrates this. Its substance is as follows:—

"The drops of water on the surface of the ocean looked up at the fleecy clouds passing over the face of the sky, and ardently longed to leave the dull leaden depths and soar with ease in their company. So they determined to *try*.

"They called upon the wind to help them. It blew fiercely, and the frantic waves flung themselves in all their force against the rocks until it seemed as if the drops, now broken into fine spray, *must* reach to the clouds and stop there. But no! back at last they fell in fine showers upon the cold, dark waves. At last they sighed and said 'It never will be.' The wind dropped and the storm was over.

"Then it was that the sun shone forth in its strength, the sea lay placid beneath its hot rays, and lo! almost ere they knew it, the drops were lifted by its mighty power, and without noise or effort they found themselves floating away as vapour into the blue sky."

Deliverance is even thus. Keep in the warm sunshine of the love of Christ to you, and soon you will be saying, "I thank God through Jesus Christ our Lord" (Rom. 7:25).

Chapter Thirteen

SAFETY AND SANCTIFICATION

When God called Israel out of Egypt, the first thing He did was to ensure their safety from judgment by sheltering them beneath the blood of the slain lamb. Next, to sanctify the firstborn who had been sheltered. Exodus 12 gives us details of the one, and Exodus 13 starts with the other. "Sanctify unto Me all the firstborn."

This is the Old Testament type, and in the New Testament safety and sanctification are again connected. In John 17, for instance, the Lord Jesus declared the *safety* of His own. As to the *past*, He said, "Those that Thou gavest Me I have kept." As to the *future*, He prayed, "Holy Father, keep through Thine own name those whom Thou hast given Me" (verses 11 and 12). Immediately following this He prayed concerning their sanctification (verses 17 and 19).

With these scriptures before us, we shall see that it is God's wish that the believer should be both safe and sanctified. Let us not, however, connect our safety with our growth in grace, neither let us so widely separate them as to make them a first and second blessing, with possibly years of experience rolling between. To understand the proper relation between safety and sanctification we need to know the scriptural meaning of the terms, and upon what each of them depends.

No one who reads these lines will have any difficulty as to what is meant by "safety." With "sanctification" it may be otherwise. Not many words in the Scriptures are more widely misunderstood.

To some sanctification means *sanctimoniousness*. It really means nothing of the sort; nor does it even mean *becoming very holy*, save in a secondary sense. The primary meaning of sanctify is to *set apart* — to separate from base uses to the service and pleasure of God. For example:—

"Thou shalt anoint the altar . . . and sanctify the altar . . . thou shalt anoint the laver . . . and sanctify it" (Exod. 40:10,11).

"I [Jesus] sanctify Myself" (John 17:19).

"Sanctify the Lord God in your hearts" (1 Peter 3:15).

In what sense can an object constructed of wood or metal be said to be sanctified? It cannot be made *holy* in the ordinary sense of that word. Inanimate objects have no qualities of mind or character. They can, however, be solemnly *set apart* for divine use. Moses did so set altar and laver apart, and they were thereby sanctified or made holy in the Scripture use of the term.

Again, how can we conceive of God Himself or the Lord Jesus as being *sanctified*, in whose presence the angels cover their faces crying, "Holy, Holy, Holy is the Lord of Hosts"? In this same sense alone the Lord Jesus has *set* Himself *apart* in heaven for our sakes, and we can *set* God Himself *apart* in our hearts, ever giving Him that place of supremacy and honour which is His by right.

So, too, when sanctification is connected with us believers, it has just this primary meaning. The above-quoted scripture, Exodus 13:2, shows that sanctification is God claiming for Himself those whom He has sheltered by blood. We are thereby separated, or set apart, for the pleasure and service of God.

We must carefully note, however, that for us sanctification has two aspects. The first *positional* and *absolute* — an act of God with which we start our Christian career; the second *practical* and *progressive* — continuing and deepening through all our pathway upon earth.

Those scriptures, which speak of the believer as having been already sanctified, naturally fall under our first heading. For instance, Paul wrote to the Corinthians in his first epistle as unto "them that are sanctified in Christ Jesus" (1:2). And again, "But ye are washed, but ye are sanctified, but ye are justified in the name of the Lord Jesus, and by the Spirit of our God" (6:11). These are striking sayings, for the Corinthian Christians were in many respects very blameworthy. They had not advanced far in the way of *practical* sanctification, yet the apostle does not hesitate to remind them that in the name of the Lord Jesus and by God's Spirit they *had been* sanctified as truly as they had been washed and justified. They had been set apart for God.

Again, in Hebrews 10 we read, "By one offering He hath perfected for ever them that are sanctified" (verse 14). Who are these sanctified ones? Are they believers of special attainments in holiness? *No*. They are all Christians without distinction or class — set apart for God in virtue of the one sacrifice of our Lord Jesus Christ.

But there are other scriptures where sanctification *is* presented as an object of attainment and desire. We read, "This is the will of God, even your sanctification" (1 Thess. 4:3). "Christ loved the church, and gave Himself for it; that He might sanctify and cleanse it" (Eph. 5:25,26). "If a man therefore purge himself from these, he shall be a vessel unto honour, sanctified and meet for the Master's use" (2 Tim. 2:21).

In these scriptures, though sanctification still carries its root meaning of "setting apart," it is clearly viewed as something which is God's intention for His people; as something which Christ — not has done — but *is doing* for His church to-day; as something which we are to individually seek, and which, instead of being already ours by God's gracious act, is to be ours if we respond to the divine instructions. In a word, it is sanctification of a practical and progressive sort.

Now let us inquire, upon what do these things depend? *Safety*, in Scripture, ever stands related to the infinite worth and value of the atoning work of Christ, and to His power to keep. Our attainments in practical holiness after conversion, important as they are in their place, have nothing to say to it. On that fateful night in Egypt no firstborn son would have been spared if the head of the household had tacked a paper to the lintel of the door, narrating his boy's excellences of character or his progress in holy behaviour. The safety of every spared firstborn depended solely upon the sprinkled blood and on nothing else. So it is for us. Our safety, our forgiveness and justification hang entirely upon the precious blood of Christ. We are forgiven "through His name" (Acts 10:43), we are justified "by His blood" (Rom. 5:9).

But upon what does *sanctification* depend? In its positional aspect it is founded on the work of Christ. By His one offering we are sancti-fied. It also stands connected with the Holy Spirit. We are "elect . . . through sanctification of the Spirit" (1 Peter 1:2). By the Spirit we are born again, and finally, in believing the truth, we are sealed by that same Spirit. In virtue of all this, we are set apart for God.

In its practical and progressive aspect sanctification depends upon the truth. "Sanctify them through Thy truth; Thy word is truth" (John 17:17). Hence the sanctifying of Ephesians 5:26 is "by the Word." This being so, it is easy to see that diligence, and purpose of heart in departing from iniquity, are very necessary in this connection. If we "walk in the Spirit" (Gal. 6:16) we do not fulfil the wishes of the flesh. Christ is before us as our Object, and we are brought under the influence of the truth of the Word, and thereby practically set apart for God in mind and affections. This practical sanctification goes on through all our pilgrim days.

If we disconnect safety and sanctification, will not people think they may be saved and yet live as they like?

We will not disconnect them; far from it. Scripture makes it abundantly plain that those whom God shelters from judgment, He separates unto Himself. That one should be sheltered and yet left in the world under the power of sin, is simply unthinkable to the Christian mind. The unregenerate alone would entertain such an idea.

But though we do *not* disconnect we do distinguish, for Scripture does so. Some there are who hopelessly confuse these two things. In their great desire to keep us humble and walking in the way that is right, they would have us believe that the degree of our attainments in practical sanctification determines the degree of our safety.

Is this so? Is our sanctification of such a doubtful character that we must be kept in perilous uncertainty lest we should shatter it? Let an analogy answer. Is it necessary to terrify little children in order to make them behave themselves? Is this method — sometimes practised by ignorant nursery-maids — the *only* way to reach that desirable end, or even the *best* way? Why then should we suppose that God treats His children on such lines? The truth is that all right conduct flows from the knowledge that we *are* sheltered, and from the right understanding of *what* we are separated to.

Does good progress in practical sanctification
improve the believer's title to a place in heaven?

Not in the smallest degree, though without holiness no man shall
see the Lord. Near the close of his strenuous life, marked by so high a
degree of holy living and devoted service, the apostle Paul wrote: "to
depart and to be with Christ; which is far better" (Phil. 1:23). To a dying
robber, just converted, but without many hours of holy living to his
credit, Jesus said, "To-day shalt thou be with Me in paradise" (Luke
23:43).

Which of these two had the better prospects of heaven — that
heaven which is summed up in the words "with Christ," "with Me"?
Paul? Nay, their prospects were good alike, and as sure and firm as the
finished work of Christ and the sure Word of God could make them.

Fitness for heaven is not something the believer works up to — he
starts with it. We give thanks to the Father "who *hath* made us meet to be
partakers of the inheritance of the saints in light" (Col. 1:12). HATH,
mark you! It is not something He is doing, but something that *He has
done*.

Good progress in practical sanctification does, however, improve
our *fitness for earth*! We are thereby rendered much more able to take
our proper place as witnesses and servants of Christ in this world.

When does this progressive or practical sanctification take place? Do we receive it by an act of
faith?

It is impossible to name a certain day or hour and say, "Then I was
sanctified in a practical sense." For then, how could it be progressive?
Nor do we receive it by an *act* of faith. Faith, of course, there must be,
faith in the fact that we are already set apart by God for Himself. And
faith is not an *act* merely to which we attain by a kind of supreme effort.
Faith truly *acts*, but it is itself an abiding and continuous thing. I
believed. Yes, but I *do* believe. I believe to-day!

Taking Scripture as our guide we learn that the Truth sanctifies,
and that God's Word is truth (John 17:17). Further, that the Spirit of God
sanctifies. He is the sanctifying power, inasmuch as He it is who guides

us into all truth (John 16:13). The truth presents CHRIST to us, it opens out to our souls His glory, and as by faith we behold Him we are changed into His image, from one degree of glory to another (2 Cor. 3:17,18). That is progressive sanctification indeed!

Can you tell us when a Christian is entitled to speak of himself as sanctified?

Every true believer *is* sanctified. To each it can be said, "Of Him are ye in Christ Jesus, who of God is made unto us wisdom, and righteousness, and sanctification, and redemption" (1 Cor. 1:30). So that, if truly converted and "in Christ Jesus," you may speak of yourself as sanctified with as much confidence as you would speak of yourself as redeemed.

If, however, your question refers to practical sanctification, the answer is — *Never!* Those in whom the largest measure of sanctification is found, who — in other words — are most Christ-like, are the last people in the world to say so. CHRIST, and not attainments, fills the vision of their souls. The excellency of the knowledge of Christ Jesus their Lord (*see* Phil. 3:8) is their pursuit as it was Paul's, and if they speak of themselves at all it is to say, "*Not as though I had already attained, either were already perfect*" (Phil. 3:12).

We read in Scripture about the believer being sanctified wholly. Would not such a believer be perfect and beyond the reach of temptation?

People who do not observe the setting of scriptural expressions, sometimes suppose that to be sanctified wholly is to have the old nature completely eradicated. A glance at the passage will, however, help us to seize the meaning of these words. It runs thus:—

"Abstain from all appearance of evil. And the very God of peace sanctify you wholly; and I pray God your whole spirit and soul and body be preserved blameless unto the coming of our Lord Jesus Christ" (1 Thess. 5:22,23).

The apostle Paul desired, in regard to each of his converts, that the whole man might be practically set apart for God. Each of the three parts that go to make up a man — spirit, soul, and body — was to be affected, and to such an extent that he not only kept separate from evil, but also from all appearance of it. Nothing less than this should be the object of our prayerful desire even now. But "if we say that we have no sin, we deceive ourselves, and the truth is not in us" (1 John 1:8). It goes without saying that if the old nature be not eradicated, no believer can consider himself perfect or beyond the reach of temptation.

Why does the Bible lay such stress on this positional or absolute sanctification which all believers possess to begin with? Of what practical benefit is it to us?

It is of the greatest possible importance. The law may, indeed, set before us an ideal to which we are to strive to attain. God's way in grace is to show us what we ARE in His own sovereign choice, that we may practically be consistent with it.

Two boys are born on the self-same day: one is the son of a king, set apart from his birth to high estate and office; the other is the son of a pauper. Why is it that continually the young prince has it impressed upon him that he is the son of a king? Is there any practical benefit in it? Indeed there is. The two boys may often walk the same streets, but their practical life and behaviour are as different as can be. The prince is practically separated from many low and vulgar ways, because by birth he was absolutely set apart to kingly estate.

So it must ever be with us. Never can we be too often reminded that by the redemption work of Christ, by the Spirit's work and indwelling, we *have been* set apart for God. Nothing will prove more truly conducive to holy living.

Chapter Fourteen

LAW AND GRACE

There are two verses which shed such light upon this subject that we must quote them at once.

"The law was given by Moses, but grace and truth came by Jesus Christ" (John 1:17).

"Sin shall not have dominion over you: for ye are not under the law, but under grace" (Rom. 6:14).

The first of these shows us the great dispensational change which took place at the coming of Christ. The second, the result of that change so far as the believer is concerned. Under the new regime he obtains freedom from the slavery of sin.

In one respect law and grace are alike. Both set before us a very exalted standard — though even in this the latter excels. In all other respects they are exact opposites.

At Mount Sinai the law of Moses was given (Exod. 19,20). God — but very little known, because still hidden in thick darkness — then laid down explicitly His righteous and holy demands. If men obeyed they were blessed: if they disobeyed they came under the law's solemn curse (Gal. 3:10). As a matter of fact the law was broken and the curse merited before there was time for the tables of stone to reach the people (Exod. 32). The succeeding chapter tells us how God dealt in mercy with them. Under law not tempered by mercy they must have instantly perished.

Grace, on the other hand, means that God having fully revealed Himself to us in His Son, all His righteous and holy demands have been met in Christ's death and resurrection, so that blessing is available for *all*. To *all who believe* forgiveness of sins and the gift of the Spirit are granted, so that there may be power to conform them to the standard — which under grace is nothing short of Christ Himself.

The very essence of law, then, is *demand*, that of grace is *supply*.

Under law God, so to speak, stands before us saying, "*Give!* render to Me your love and dutiful obedience." Under grace He stands with full hand outstretched, saying, "*Take!* receive of My love and saving power."

Law says, "Do and live," grace says, "Live and do."

Now we believers, as we have seen, are not under law, but under grace. Let us see how that has come to pass. Galatians 4:4,5 will tell us:—

"When the fulness of the time was come, God sent forth His Son, made of a woman, made under the law, to redeem them that were under the law, that we might receive the adoption of sons."

That which has made the change is in one word, *redemption*. But that involved the death of the Redeemer. He must needs be made a curse for us by dying on the tree (Gal. 3:13). Hence it is that the believer is entitled to regard himself as "dead to the law" (Rom. 7:4). He died in the death of his Representative, the Lord Jesus Christ. The law did not die; on the contrary, never was its majesty so upheld as when Jesus died beneath its curse. Two things, however, did happen. First, the law being magnified and its curse borne, God suspends His wrath, and proclaims *grace* to all mankind. Second, the believer died to the law in the Person of his great Representative. He is, to use the Scripture language, "married to Another, even to Him who is raised from the dead" (Rom. 7:4), *i.e.*, he is now controlled by another Power, and that power is in a *Person* — the risen Son of God.

Connected with these two things are two great facts.

First, *the law is not the ground of a sinner's justification.* He is justified by grace, by the blood of Christ, by faith. This is fully reasoned out in Romans 3 and 4. Second, *the law is not the rule of life for the believer.* Christ is that. Our links are with Him and not with law, as we have seen (Rom. 7:4). This is fully shown in Galatians 3 and 4.

The Galatian Christians had started well, converted under the preaching of the Gospel of the *grace* of God by the Apostle. Then came along the Judaizing mischief-makers, who were "zealous of the law," and taught circumcision and law-keeping. Into this snare the Galatians fell.

Paul's answer is virtually this, that the law was a provisional arrangement (3:17), brought in to show up Israel's transgressions (verse 19), and acting as a schoolmaster "up to Christ" (verse 24), as it should read. Christ being come, redemption having been accomplished, and the Spirit having been given, the believer leaves the position of a child under age, or that of a servant, and becomes a son in the Divine household, being thus put in the liberty of grace (6:1–7).

Inasmuch as the grace platform, on to which we have been lifted, is much higher than the law platform which we have left, to go back even in mind from the one to the other is to *fall*. "Ye are fallen from grace" is the Apostle's word to such as do this.

The parable of the prodigal son illustrates the point. His highest thought did not rise above law, when he said, "Make me as one of thy hired servants." He was received, however, in pure grace, and the son's place inside was given. Suppose, however, that a few days after, under the plea of wishing to retain his father's affection and the place and privileges so freely bestowed, he had commenced working as a household drudge and rigidly conforming himself to the laws which governed the servants, what then? He would have "fallen from grace," and sadly grieved the heart of his father, since it would have been equivalent to a vote of "no confidence" in him.

How important, then, for us to have the heart "established with grace" (Heb. 13:9).

What do you say to the idea that grace came in to help us to keep the law, so that we might go to heaven that way?

Simply this — that it is totally opposed to Scripture. In the first place, the idea that keeping the law entitles a person to heaven is a fallacy. When the lawyer asked the Lord, "What shall I do to inherit eternal life?" he was referred to the law, and upon giving a correct summary of its demands, Jesus answered, "Thou hast answered right; this do, and thou shalt *live*" (Luke 10:25–28). There is not a word about going to heaven. *Life upon earth is the reward of law-keeping.*

Then, secondly, grace came in not to help us keep the law, but to bring us salvation from its curse by Another bearing it for us. Galatians 3 plainly shows this.

If, however, further confirmation be required, read Romans 3, and notice that when law has convicted and closed man's mouth (verses 9–19), grace through righteousness justifies *"without the law"* (verses 20–24).

Read also 1 Timothy 1. Law is made to convict the ungodly (verses 9,10). The Gospel of grace presents Christ Jesus who "came into the world to *save sinners*" (verse 15). Not, be it noted, to help sinners to keep the law, and so attempt to save themselves.

If the law was not given for us to keep, and so be justified, what was it given for?

Let Scripture itself answer:— "What things soever the law saith, it saith . . . *that every mouth may be stopped, and all the world may become guilty before God*" (Rom. 3:19), "The law entered, *that the offence might abound*" (Rom. 5:20).

"Wherefore then serveth the law? *It was added because of transgressions*" (Gal. 3:19).

The law has, like every other institution of God, signally achieved its purpose. It can convict and silence the most obstinately self-conceited religionist. Grace alone can save him.

Then has grace set aside the law and annulled it for ever?

Grace, personified in Jesus, has borne the curse of the broken law, thereby redeeming all who believe from its *curse* (Gal. 3:13).

Further, it has redeemed us from under *the law itself*, and placed all our relationships with God on a new footing (Gal. 4:4–6).

Now if the believer is no longer under law, but under grace, we must not suppose that the law itself is either annulled or set aside. Its majesty was never more clearly upheld than when the righteous One suffered as a Substitute under its curse, and multitudes will quail before its impeachment at the day of judgment (Rom. 2:12).

What harm is there in a Christian adopting the law as a rule of life?

A great deal. By so doing he "falls from grace," for grace teaches as well as saves (Titus 2:11–14).

He also lowers the Divine standard. Not law but Christ is the standard for the believer.

He further gets hold of the wrong motive power. Fear may impel a person to attempt, though unsuccessfully, to keep the law, and regulate the power of the "flesh" within. The Spirit of God is the power that does control the flesh and conform to Christ (Gal. 5:16–18).

Lastly, he does violence to the relationships in which he stands by the grace of God. Though a son in the liberty of the Father's house and heart, he insists on putting himself under the code of rules drawn up for the regulation of the servants' hall!

Is there no harm in all this? We venture to say there is.

If you teach that the Christian is not under the law, may it not lead to all kinds of wickedness?

It would, IF a person became a Christian without the new birth, or repentance, without coming under the influence of grace and receiving the gift of the Holy Spirit.

Since, however, no one is a Christian without these things, the case wears a different aspect, and to reason in the way suggested only betrays deplorable ignorance of the truth of the Gospel.

The argument simply comes to this: that the only way to make Christians live holy lives is to keep them under the threat of the law, as if they had only a kind of sow-nature, and the only way to keep them out of the mire is to drive them back with sticks. The truth is that though the flesh is still within the believer, he has also the new nature, and it is with *that* that God identifies him. He has the Spirit of Christ to lead him, and hence he may be safely put under grace; for after all it is grace that subdues.

If people quarrel with this, their quarrel is with the Scripture quoted at first.

"Sin shall not have dominion over you: *for ye are not under the law, but under grace*" (Rom. 6:14).

Unconverted men may attempt to use grace as a cloak for wickedness, but that is no reason for denying the truth stated in that verse. What truth is there which has not been abused by evil men?

Does Scripture indicate how grace keeps the believer in order, so that he may please God?

It does. Titus 2:11–15 supplies the answer. In Christianity grace not only saves but teaches, and what an effective teacher it is! It does not fill our heads with cold rules or regulations, but brings our hearts under the subduing influence of the love of God. We learn what is pleasing to Him as set forth in Jesus, and having the Spirit we begin to live the sober, righteous, and godly life.

There is a very great difference between a family of children kept in order by fear of the birch upon misbehaviour and those who live in a home where love rules. Order *may* reign in the former, but it will end in a big explosion ere the children come to years. In the latter there is not only obedience, but a joyful response to the parents' desires, the fruit of responsive affection.

God rules His children on the love principle, and not on the birch-rod principle.

May we live our lives in the happy consciousness of this!

Chapter Fifteen

"SIN" AND "SINS."

We have no love for theological hair-splitting, and we shall certainly not be guilty of it in carefully distinguishing between these two things. Though closely connected, there is an important difference between them.

Both are mentioned in one verse of Scripture, Romans 5:12. "By one man sin entered into the world, and death by sin; and so death passed upon all men, for that all have sinned."

"*Sin*" is that which at the fall of Adam gained an entrance into the world. Just as the poison of a snake, once injected into a man's body, will run through his whole system doing its deadly work, so sin — the virus of that old serpent the devil — has permeated man's moral being to his ruin. The result of this is "all have sinned." "Sins," of thought, word, or act, whether of omission or commission, are chargeable to each of us.

"Sin," then, is the root principle; "sins" the shameful fruits that spring therefrom.

This being granted, let us go a step further and ask, what exactly is this "sin" which has entered into the world?

1 John 3:4 answers this point, but, unfortunately, it is one of the verses where our excellent Authorized Version leads us astray. The one Greek word translated by the phrase "transgression of the law" really means "lawlessness," and is so translated in other Versions. The verse, then, should run thus, "Whosoever committeth sin practises lawlessness; for *sin is lawlessness*."

There is an immense difference between these two things. "Transgression of the law" is, indeed, the breaking of a clear-cut commandment. There can be no transgression of the law where there is no law to transgress. There was no law in the world from Adam until the days of Moses, hence there was no transgression and sin was not imputed; yet sin was there in awful malignancy, and death its penalty was there. This is just the argument of Romans 5:13, 14.

What, then, is lawlessness? It is simply the refusal of all rule, the throwing off of all divine restraint. The assertion of man's will in defiance of God's. Sin is just *that*. Such was the course to which Adam committed himself in eating the forbidden fruit. How bitter the results!

Instead of being like a planet, shining with steady light, and moving evenly onward in its orbit, controlled by the sun, man has become like a "wandering star," pursuing an erratic course he knows not where; though Scripture significantly says "to whom is reserved the blackness of darkness for ever" (Jude 13).

Instead of being master, he is mastered by the evil thing to which he has yielded himself. Sin has dominion over him and continually breaks out into sins. And, sad to say, it exerts such a deadening and stupefying influence upon the conscience that sinners seem unconscious of their plight apart from the grace of God.

When God's grace does act, and the Spirit works in life-giving power in a soul, the first cry is that of need and pain. The past years rise up before it, burdening the conscience. SINS become the question of the hour, and the trouble does not cease until the value of the precious blood of Christ is known and the soul can say, "My sins are forgiven me for His name's sake."

Then, afterwards — this is undoubtedly the experience of most believers — the question of SIN is raised. We discover that though our sins are forgiven, the root principle from which the mischief springs is still within us. What is to be done with that? This is a question indeed.

It is something gained if we discern that SIN lies at the root of our troubles. Some Christians seem to be too much occupied with the fruit to consider the root.

Some years ago a youth approached an elder Christian, complaining that in spite of all his prayers and efforts sins were continually creeping into his life and behaviour. SINS, SINS, was the burden of his cry!

"Upon what tree do apples grow?" was the only answer he got.

"Why, an apple tree," said the astonished youth. The question seemed so ridiculously irrelevant.

"And on what tree do plums grow?"

"On a plum tree." His astonishment deepened!

"And on what tree do sins grow?" was the next question.

A pause. Then, with a smile, he said, "On a sin tree, I should think."

"You are right, my lad," said this friend. "That's just where they do grow."

Note the point. The sins that we Christians have to deplore and confess are not little isolated bits of evil foreign to us, inserted somehow into our lives by the devil. Their cause lies much deeper. They spring as fruit out of that which is within us. Sin is within us. Let no man say otherwise when Scripture says, "If we say that we have no sin, we deceive ourselves, and the truth is not in us" (1 John 1:8).

What, then, is the remedy for SIN? The answer is, in one word, DEATH.

Death, or better still, the resurrection change, which will be the portion of us, who are alive and remain when Jesus comes. It will end sin as far as we are concerned, absolutely and for ever. The last trace of its presence in us will then be gone. Every Christian looks *on* in the happy anticipation of that. Do we all as joyfully look *back* to the hour when death the great remedy came in — the death of Jesus?

"In that He died, He died unto sin once; but in that He liveth, He liveth unto God" (Rom. 6:10).

The matter, therefore, stands thus: He died FOR *our sins*, atoning for them; He died TO *sin*, and therefore taught by the Spirit we recognize that we are identified with our great Representative, and faith appropriates His death as ours. We, too, then, are "dead to sin," and cannot any longer consistently live in it (*see* Rom. 6:2). We therefore reckon ourselves "to be dead indeed unto sin, but alive unto God through Jesus Christ our Lord" (Rom. 6:11).

There is just this difference: the sin to which He died was purely an external thing.

"In Him is no sin" (1 John 3:5). With us it is not only external, but internal too. Sin is the ruling principle of the world without us; it is also, alas! the ruling principle of the flesh within.

But there is more than this. The death of Christ was not only our death to sin, but it was the total condemnation of the sin to which we died. Romans 8:3 runs, "God sending His own Son in the likeness of sinful flesh, and by a sacrifice for sin [*margin*] condemned sin in the flesh." At the Cross SIN, in its full hideousness, stood revealed, for lawlessness reached its flood-tide heights then; and in that holy sacrifice its judgment was borne, and its condemnation expressed.

Let these distinctions, then, be carefully noted. *Sins* have been borne and their judgment exhausted. *Sin* has been exposed and condemned, and to it we have died in the death of Christ. The Cross was all this and more. What heavenly wonders encircle it! How does it stand alone, unapproached and unapproachable!

> ". . . . the Tree
> Centre of two eternities,
> Which look with rapt adoring eyes
> Onward and back to Thee."

We read in John 1:29 of "the sin of the world," and in Romans 8:3 of "sin in the flesh." Is there any difference between these two? and how do you distinguish them from the sins of an individual?

The expression "sin of the world," in John 1, is about as comprehensive as can be. Sin, the root of it, and every offshoot, down to its finest ramifications in the world, is to be taken away by the Lamb of God. His Cross is the basis of it, and He Himself will do it, as foretold in Revelation 19–21.

"Sin in the flesh" is somewhat different. Sin is, of course, the same in essence wherever it is found in the universe of God, whether in demons or men, but as far as this world is concerned "the flesh" — the old fallen nature of the children of Adam — is the great vehicle in which it resides and works, producing sins in individuals universally.

Picture to yourself an immense electric-power station. Imagine a whole network of live wires, quite unprotected, radiating in every direction from it all over a vast city. Shocks, consternation, death, would be in every direction!

Sin is something like the subtle and indefinable electric fluid making its influence felt in every direction.

The flesh is like the wire, the seat of the electricity, and the vehicle through which it acts.

Sins are like the shocks dealt out in every direction, resulting in *death*.

The sin of the world is like the whole concern, wires, electricity, power-station and all! A clean sweep of the hateful thing will be made. Such is the value of the Cross. Well might John say, "Behold the Lamb of God!"

We commonly speak of the forgiveness of sins. Might we not as correctly speak of the forgiveness of sin?

No; for Scripture does not speak so. Forgiveness of *sins* is found continually in the Bible, forgiveness of *a sin*, too, forgiveness of *sin*, the root principle, *Never!*

A simple illustration may help. A mother is greatly tried by her little son, who is rapidly developing a most ungovernable temper. One morning, irritated because his sister is far more interested in her doll than in the motor-car which stands throbbing outside the house, he attempts to make her look at it, and in the struggle brings her head with a crash against the window, shattering the glass, and severely scratching her face.

The boy is sent to his room by his mother, and on his father's return, shortly after, he gets very properly punished.

By evening the punishment has had its desired effect. He comes to his parents in tears, confessing his wrong. Seeing that he is thoroughly repentant they forgive the angry act. But do they forgive the evil temper from which it sprang? By no means. That would be, more or less, to condone it. No; they strongly condemn it. They lovingly, yet firmly, show him its nature and its consequences, and they seek to lead him to abhor and condemn it as thoroughly as they do.

"God ... condemned sin in the flesh." He did not condone nor forgive it; and the work of the Holy Spirit in us leads us to condemn it, even as God has condemned it, to the end that we may know deliverance from its power.

How do you reconcile the condemnation of sin in the flesh with the fact that believers may and do sin?

No reconciliation is needed. *Condemnation* is not *eradication*. The same Bible that speaks of the condemnation of sin (Rom. 8:3) also speaks of the fact of sin being still in us (1 John 1:8), and supposes that the believer may sin, in pointing out the divine provision for such a case (1 John 2:1). It even plainly tells us that as a matter of fact we all do sin (James 3:2).

It is God's way to leave the flesh and sin still in the believer, that, practically learning their true nature, he may experimentally come into line with God's condemnation of them at the Cross, and find his life and deliverance in Another, so that he can say, in answer to the cry, "Who shall deliver me?", "I thank God, through Jesus Christ our Lord" (Rom. 7:24,25).

Is sin never taken completely out of a believer? It says in 1 John 3:9, "Whosoever is born of God doth not commit sin."

At death, when a believer is "absent from the body and present with the Lord," he is done with sin for ever. At the Lord's coming all believers will get their glorified bodies without one trace of sin being there. Until then we have the presence of sin in us, though it is our privilege to be delivered from its power.

The verse quoted does not in the least conflict with the other Scriptures we have considered. It simply states for us the *nature* of the one born of God. He does not practise sin. ("Practise" rather than "commit" is the real force of the word here). It is not his nature so to do. In so saying the apostle viewed believers in their nature as born of God, without reference to any qualifying feature, which may assert itself in the wear and tear of life.

For instance, a man might walk along the sea-front of some fishing-village with a friend, and, pointing to a large net with innumerable cork-floats attached, say, "What a great boon to the fisherman is a substance like cork, which cannot sink." "Indeed," says his friend, "it can, for only an hour ago I watched the men recovering that very net from the bottom of the sea; the weights attached to the under side were too heavy, and, overcoming the buoyancy of the cork, dragged the whole lot down."

Who was right? Both were, allowing for their respective points of view. The former was thinking of the abstract qualities of cork, the latter of a curious and abnormal thing that happened in practice.

The apostle John writes from the abstract point of view, and sin in a Christian is certainly not a *normal*, but a most *abnormal* thing!

Christians, however, do sin all too frequently. Do such sins do away with the settlement reached both as to sin and sins, with which the Christian starts?

No. The cross of Christ is the ground of all. There *sin* was condemned. There atonement was made, so that forgiveness reaches us when we believe. All, too, is the gift of divine grace, and "the gifts and calling of God are without repentance" (Rom. 11:29), *i.e.* they are not subject to a change of mind on God's part. They are for ever.

Sins after conversion do, however, greatly upset the Christian's happiness, and dispel the joy both of forgiveness and relationship with God, until in self-judgment such sins are confessed, and through the advocacy of Christ we get the Father's forgiveness (*see* 1 John 1:9; 2:1). Painful lessons in this way we all have to learn, but there is profit in them. We discover thus the true nature of the flesh within us, and that the only way to keep from gratifying its desire is to "walk in the Spirit" (Gal. 5:16).

Did the Lord Jesus Christ in dying bear the sins of everybody? Would not that follow from the fact that He takes away the sin of the world, according to John 1:29?

Scripture puts things thus:
"He died for all" (2 Cor. 5:15).
"Who gave Himself a ransom for all" (1 Tim. 2:6).
"He is the propitiation for our sins; and not for ours only, but also for the sins of the whole world" (1 John 2:2).

These verses indicate what we may call the Godward aspect of His work. It includes ALL within the wide sweep of its benevolent intention; and propitiation has been made on behalf, not only of believers, but everybody; the whole world.

When we come, not to the *intention* or *bearing* of His work, but its actual *results*, we find things put differently. When we view things on the largest possible scale, and "think imperially," in the best sense of the word, John 1:29 does indeed apply, but that is quite in keeping with the fact that sin and all that are eternally identified with it find their part in the lake of fire.

If we think of things in detail, we cannot say He bore the sins of everybody, for Scripture says:

"Who His own self bare *our* [*i.e.* believers'] sins in His own body on the tree" (1 Peter 2:27).

Hence it is that again we read:

"Christ was once offered to bear the sins of *many*" (Heb. 9:28). Thanks be to God that we find ourselves amongst them!

Chapter Sixteen

THE NEW NATURE
AND THE OLD

Many Christians experience a good deal of difficulty in daily life as a result of having no clear understanding of this subject. They are conscious of a whole host of desires and emotions of a strangely conflicting nature. The apostle James may ask the question, "Doth a fountain send forth at the same place sweet water and bitter?" They, however, seem to have no difficulty in accomplishing something of this sort; for in thought, word and action they find the strangest possible jumble of good and evil until the whole problem becomes most perplexing.

It is a great help to grasp the fact that the believer is possessed of two distinct natures, the new and the old, the one the source of every right desire, the other the source of only evil. A hen would be sorely distracted if set to mother a mixed brood of chickens and ducklings. Their natures are distinct, and hence their desires and behaviour are very opposite, but not more opposite than the two natures of which we speak. And many believers are like that hen!

When the Lord Jesus spoke to Nicodemus He insisted upon the necessity of being "born again" — "born of water and of the Spirit," and He added, "That which is born of the flesh is flesh; and that which is born of the Spirit is spirit" (John 3:6). Let us carefully consider these important words.

In the first place they plainly indicate the existence of two natures, each characterized by its source. "Flesh" is the name of the one, for it springs from the flesh; "spirit" the name of the other, for it springs from the Holy Spirit of God.

Then it is evident that we rightly speak of "flesh" as the *old* nature, for it belongs to us as coming into the world of Adam's race by natural generation; "spirit" is the *new*, and it is ours, if born of the Spirit, in new birth.

Again, these words clearly distinguish between "spirit," by which we mean the new nature, and "the Spirit," that is, the Holy Spirit of God. The former is the direct product of His wonder-working power; and never does He indwell a person in whom He has not previously wrought in new birth, producing the new nature which is "spirit." Still, it would be a great mistake to confound — as some are inclined to do — the new nature with the Holy Spirit who produces it.

When you were born again, then there was implanted in you by the Holy Spirit this new nature, which is spirit, and one of the first results of this was the inevitable clashing of this new nature with the old, which you inherited as a child of Adam. Both strive for the mastery, each pulling in a diametrically opposite direction, and until the secret of deliverance from the power of the flesh within is learned, the painful jumble of right and wrong is bound to continue.

In the seventh chapter of the Epistle to the Romans that painful experience is described for us. Carefully read it, noticing especially verses 14 to the end, and continuing your reading as far as chapter 8:4. Do you not see in it a good many features which tally with your experiences?

In that chapter the speaker reaches one very important conclusion. "I know that in me (that is, in my flesh) dwelleth no good thing" (verse 18). The flesh, then, is utterly and hopelessly bad, and God allows us to wade through the mire of bitter experiences that we may thoroughly learn this lesson. "The flesh profiteth *nothing*," are the Saviour's own words (John 6:63). "They that are in the flesh *cannot* please God," are words that corroborate the story (Rom. 8:8). This being so, out of it nothing but evil will come.

Flesh may be left uncared-for and untrained, it then becomes heathen, savage, and possibly even cannibal flesh. It may be highly refined and educated, it is now curbed, civilized, christianized flesh, but *it is flesh*, for that which is born of the flesh is flesh, no matter what you do with it. And in it — high-class flesh though it be — *no good dwells*.

What can you do with a nature like that, a nature which is simply the vehicle of sin, in which sin dwells and works? Let us answer that question by asking another. What has God done with it? what is His remedy?

Romans 8:3 supplies the answer: "For what the law could not do, in that it was weak through the flesh, God, sending His own Son in the likeness of sinful flesh and for sin, condemned sin in the flesh."

The law from the beginning strongly censured the flesh, but it could neither curb it nor control it so that we might be delivered from its power. But what the law could not do God has done. In the cross of Christ He judicially dealt with it, "condemned sin in the flesh," *i.e.*, He condemned it in the very root and essence of its nature.

Romans 8:4 gives the practical result of this. The cross being the condemnation of the old nature in the root of its being, we have received the Holy Spirit to be the power of the new nature, so that walking in the Spirit we fulfil all the righteous requirements of the law, though no longer under it as our rule of life.

God then has *condemned*, in the cross of Christ, the flesh — the old nature. But what can we do with it? We can thankfully accept what God has done, and treat it henceforward as a condemned thing ourselves. The apostle Paul indicates this when he says, "We are the circumcision, which worship God in the Spirit, and rejoice in Christ Jesus, and have NO CONFIDENCE in the flesh" (Phil. 3:3).

When one reads this scripture commenceing so positively with the words "We are," one is inclined to ask, "*Are we?*" Am I so thoroughly alive to the *true character* of the flesh — no good thing dwelling in it, on the one hand, and *God's condemnation* of it in the cross, on the other — that I have *no confidence* in it, even in its fairest forms? Depend upon it, here lies the crux of the whole matter. That point is not easily reached. Many a painful experience is passed through, many a heart-breaking failure is known, as again and again the flesh, like a Samson refusing to be bound, snaps the seven green withs of pious and prayerful efforts, and the new ropes — so carefully woven — of good resolutions. But when once it really is reached the battle is well-nigh over.

The shattering of our confidence in the flesh is largely the shattering of the flesh's power over us. Then at once we look away from ourselves, and our most earnest efforts, for a Deliverer, and find Him in the Lord

Jesus Christ, who has taken possession of us by His Spirit. The Spirit is the power; He not only checkmates the activity of the old nature (*see* Gal. 5:16), but energizes, expands and controls the new (*see* Rom. 8:2,4,5, and 10).

Bear in mind that the new nature has no power *in itself.* Romans 7 shows that. The new nature in itself gives aspirations and desires which are right and beautiful, but for power to fulfil them there must be this practical submission to Christ and His Spirit — this walking in the Spirit, which is largely the result of coming into real and heartfelt agreement with God's condemnation of the old nature in the cross of Christ.

Some people are good-natured and religious almost from birth. Do such need the new nature of which you speak?

Most certainly they do. The very man to whom the Lord Jesus uttered those memorable words, "YE MUST be born again," was exactly of that type. Morally, socially, and religiously, everything was in his favour, yet the Lord met him point-blank, not only with an abstract proposition (John 3:3), but with the same truth in concrete and pointedly personal form. "Ye must be born again" (verse 7).

That settles it. After all, good-natured and religious flesh is only FLESH, and will not do for God.

There is a widespread idea that everybody has some spark of good in him, and that it only needs developing by prayer and self-control. Is this scriptural?

It is very *un*scriptural, indeed it is *anti*scriptural. Many passages might be cited, but I shall content myself with two.

The first shall be *negative* evidence. In Romans 3:9–19, we have given us a full-length portrait of mankind in its moral features. The details are culled by the apostle Paul from Old Testament Scriptures. First come sweeping general statements (verses 10–12), then incisive particular ones in hideous detail (verses 13–18), and not one word is breathed as to this latent spark of good. How unjust, how untruthful, if really, after all, it be there! The God who cannot lie describes His creatures, and does not mention this supposed spark of good. The inference is obvious. *It is not there.*

The positive evidence runs like this:—

"God saw that the wickedness of man was great in the earth; and that *every* imagination of the thoughts of his heart was *only* EVIL *continually*" (Gen. 6:5).

The apostle Paul puts the same truth in different words when he says; "I know that in me (that is, in my flesh) dwelleth *no good thing*" (Rom. 7:18) — not even *one* spark of good.

For those who believe the Bible such evidence is quite conclusive. Nothing more remains to be said.

Does a person get rid of the old at new birth, or are we to understand that a converted person has both the old and the new within him?

The old nature is not eradicated at new birth, else we should not read: "If we say that we have no sin we deceive ourselves, and the truth is not in us" (1 John 1:8).

Neither is it changed into the new nature. New birth is not like the philosopher's stone, which was fabled to turn every object it touched into fine gold. John 3:6, already quoted proves this.

Both natures are *in* the believer just as both natures are in that standard fruit tree in the garden. Indeed, the process of "grafting" not inaptly illustrates the matter in hand, for by it the wild stock into which the choice and cultivated apple shoot is inserted is condemned. The knife is put to it and it is cut hard back for the process to take place. Further, instantly the graft is made the gardener no longer recognizes it as a wild stock, but calls it by the name of the apple variety he has grafted in.

So it is for us; both natures are there, yet God only recognizes the new, and we, having received the Holy Spirit, are "not in the flesh, but in the Spirit" (Rom. 8:9).

If the old nature is still there, surely we must do something. How should we treat it?

We are not, of course, to be insensible to its presence, nor unaffected by its activities in us, but at the same time no amount of human resolution or effort against it will avail us.

Our wisdom is to fall into line with God's thoughts and to treat it as He does. Begin by recognizing that you are now identified with the new nature and entitled to disown the old. "It is no more I that do it, but sin that dwelleth in me" (Rom. 7:17). The new nature is your true individuality, not the old, just as the cultivated apple is the tree as soon as the graft is effective.

This being so, your treatment of it is simple. The gardener keeps a sharp look-out on his newly grafted tree. If the old wild stock seeks to assert itself, and throws up suckers from the roots, he ruthlessly cuts such suckers down as soon as they appear. So do you bring the cross of Christ to bear like a sharp knife on the old nature and its sinful desires.

"Mortify therefore *your members which are upon the earth*" (Col. 3:3). The words I have emphasized answer pretty much to the suckers thrown up by the wild stock. What they are the remainder of verse 5 and also verses 8 and 9 of the same chapter specify. Mortify them — put them to death in detail.

For this you want spiritual energy, courage, purpose of heart, which in yourself you do not possess. Your only power is in looking simply to the Lord Jesus, and placing yourself unreservedly in the hands of His Spirit.

"If ye *through the Spirit* do mortify the deeds of the body ye shall live" (Rom. 8:13).

Is it by a great act of our own will that we finally obtain the Spirit's power and overcome, or is it by yielding to God?

Let Scripture itself answer. "*Yield* yourselves unto God as those that are alive from the dead, and your members as instruments of righteousness unto God" (Rom. 6:13).

"*Yield* your members servants to righteousness unto holiness" (Rom. 6:19).

"Being made free from sin, and become *servants* to God, ye have your fruit unto holiness, and the end everlasting life" (Rom. 6:22).

The idea that the necessary power is obtained by an act of our own will looks like a last desperate attempt to obtain a little credit for the flesh somewhere, instead of totally condemning it and giving God the glory.

Does the new nature in the believer ever reach such perfect growth as to render him quite proof against the desires of the old?

2 Corinthians 12 shows very clearly that it does not. In that chapter we read that the Apostle Paul, privileged above all other Christians, was caught up into the third heaven — the immediate presence of God. After hearing there things so transporting that no human language could possibly express them, he was left to resume his ordinary life upon earth, and he tells us that God gave him from that point a thorn in the flesh — some special counter-balancing infirmity — *lest he should be exalted above measure*, through the abundance of the revelations.

Now, admittedly, Paul's Christianity was of a most advanced and extraordinary type, yet, even so, and with a temporary sojourn in the third heaven thrown in, he was not in himself proof against that self-exaltation which is inherent in the old nature.

If he was not, neither are we.

Can you give any hints that will help us to distinguish practically between desires and promptings, which spring from the old nature, and those that spring from the new?

I cannot give you any that will enable you to dispense with God's Word, and relieve you of the necessity of continually going to your knees in prayer with an exercised heart.

The Word of God it is which is "living and powerful and sharper than any two-edged sword." It alone can discern the thoughts and intents of the heart (Heb. 4:12), and the throne of grace stands ever available that we may find grace for seasonable help (Heb. 4:16). God's High Priest it is who graces that throne.

The Word of God and prayer, then, are absolutely necessary, if we would distinguish and disentangle the thoughts and desires we find within.

Recognizing this, however, it may help us if we remember that just as the mariner's compass is true to the north, so the new nature is true to God, and the old nature true to self. All that which has Christ for its object is of the one, that which has self for its object of the other.

This being so, a thousand perplexing questions would be solved by asking, "What is the secret motive which actuates me in this? Christ-glorification or self-glorification? Which?"

Chapter Seventeen

———————————

"BLOOD"
AND
"WATER."

It is an historic fact recorded by the apostle John (19:34) that a soldier with a spear pierced the side of the dead Christ, and "forthwith came there out blood and water." From the solemn way in which the Apostle pauses to attest this fact as a personal eye-witness (*see verse* 35) we might naturally conclude that he attached some very special importance to it, even if no further reference to it were made.

We are not however, left to surmise, as in his first Epistle the same apostle returns to the subject, and supplements the historic *record* of his Gospel with instructions as to the *bearing* of the fact. He says, "This is He that came by water and blood, even Jesus Christ; not by water only, but by water and blood" (verse 6). And further, in verse 8 he speaks of the Spirit and the water and the blood as the three witnesses to the Son of God.

The meaning of these words is not by any means apparent at first sight. Two things, however, do lie upon the surface.

1. Both blood and water are connected with the DEATH of Christ.

2. Though connected they are distinct, so distinct that they can be cited separately as witnesses. They must therefore, be carefully *distinguished* in our thoughts.

We find in the Scriptures that *cleansing* is connected with both blood and water, *e.g.*:—

"The blood of Jesus Christ, His Son, cleanseth us from all sin" (1 John 1:7).

"That He might sanctify it and cleanse it with the washing of water by the Word" (Eph.5:26).

Now let us seek to rightly distinguish between the two cleansings referred to. Speaking in a broad sense, we may say that they connect themselves with two great effects of sin, viz., its guilt and its defiling power.

The Blood sets before us the death of Christ in atonement for our sins, thus cancelling our guilt and bringing us forgiveness. We are thereby cleansed judicially.

The water indicates the same death, but rather as that by which our sinful state has been dealt with in judgment and ended, so as to deliver us from the old condition and associations of life in which once we lived. Thereby we are cleansed morally and the power of sin over us is broken.

Toplady was surely right when he sang:—

"Let the water and the blood,
From Thy riven side which flowed,
Be of sin the double cure,
Cleanse me from its guilt and power."

The virtue and power of the blood of Christ are set before us in Hebrews 9 and 10; indeed, the efficacy of that Blood in contrast with the inefficacy of the blood of bulls and of goats is the great theme of those chapters. We find there:—

1. The Blood of Christ purges, or cleanses the sinner's conscience from dead works to serve the living God (9:14).

2. It has removed the transgressions of saints of old, which had been for centuries accumulating under the first Covenant, *i.e.*, the Law (9:15).

3. It has ratified a new covenant of grace (9:15–18).

4. It has removed the believer's sins, and laid the basis for the putting away of sin in its totality 9:22,26).

5. It has so completely done so for faith that ONCE purged, the believer's conscience is cleared for ever so far as the judicial question of his sins is concerned (10:2).

6. It therefore gives the believer boldness to enter into the very presence of God 10:19).

7. It has once and for ever sanctified — set apart — the believer for God (10:10,29).

Bear in mind that the great subject here is the believer's access to God in virtue of the blood of Christ. His judicial clearance is perfect by that one offering, and never needs to be repeated. Hence the word which characterizes these chapters is "one," "once" (*see* 9:12,26,28; 10:2,10,12,14). Seven times over it is repeated, lest we should overlook the sufficiency and the singular glory that is connected with the precious blood of Christ.

But though judicial cleansing by Blood is the great theme of these chapters, the need for moral cleansing is not forgotten. We draw near to God having not only "our hearts sprinkled from an evil conscience," but "our bodies washed with pure water" (10:22). This is doubtless an allusion to the consecration of Aaron and his sons to the priestly office recorded in Exodus 29. They were washed with water (verse 4) as well as sprinkled with blood (verse 20). They had the shadow, we have the substance — THE DEATH OF CHRIST. It acts in both directions, as BLOOD cleansing us judicially and giving us a perfect standing before God, as WATER cleansing us morally, by cutting us off from the old life in which once we lived, and bringing us into the new.

In the very nature of things this moral cleansing by water needs to be kept up; the idea of repetition is therefore appropriate enough here. We find it so if we refer to the type. Aaron and his sons were bathed with water from head to foot at their consecration, as we have seen; *that* was not repeated, but nevertheless a laver was provided (Exod. 30:17–21), and there the priests washed their hands and feet. The instructions were most explicit: "When they go into the tabernacle of the congregation they shall wash with water, that they die not."

When we turn from type to antitype the same thought appears. In the upper chamber in Jerusalem, probably just before He instituted His supper, the Lord Jesus girded Himself, and pouring water into a basin, began to wash His disciples' feet (John 13). Peter's reluctance brings forth the truth that such washing is necessary if communion with the Lord in His heavenly position was to be enjoyed. "If I wash thee not thou hast no part with Me" (verse 8). His rapid change to enthusiastic haste leads the Lord to say: "He that is washed [*i.e.*, *bathed*] needeth not save to wash his feet, but is clean every whit" (verse 10).

Here the twofold way in which cleansing by water is presented in Scripture is very carefully distinguished. Once for all we have been "bathed." The death of Christ has cleansed us from the old life, but for all that we need the application of that death to our souls day by day. We cannot approach the sanctuary nor enjoy "part with" Christ without it.

With these thoughts before us we may perhaps return to the words quoted at the beginning from 1 John 5, and find a greater depth of meaning in them.

Jesus Christ, the Son of God, came by water and blood; by *both* these things was His coming characterized. The Spirit of God specially guards this point, saying: "*Not by water only*, but by water and blood." Why so? May not one reason be — the tendency now fast growing and ripening into apostasy, to teach that Christ did come by water only? He came, so it is now widely said, to cleanse man morally by setting before him the highest ideals, and living out those ideals Himself as an incentive to others. He came by such means to make "at-one-ment" between God and man. Such is their theory. The idea of atonement they scornfully reject.

Forseeing this dark and deadly error, the Spirit says, "not by water only, but by water and blood." Not by moral cleansing only, but by moral cleansing AND *expiation for sin*, and it is the Spirit that bears witness and "the Spirit is truth."

And so the three witnesses, the Spirit, the water, and the blood, remain: the Spirit the living acting, speaking Witness; the water and the blood two silent witnesses, and all three agree in one. They testify that He who came in this way is the Son of God, the Fountain of eternal life and that in Him eternal life is ours, who believe on the name of the Son of God.

Thanks be to God, we may fervently exclaim, that when a soldier with a spear pierced His side "forthwith came there out *blood* AND *water*"!

Has not the life-work of Christ, the mocking and scourging He suffered at men's hands, some part in His Atonement made for sins?

Precious as these are, the Scripture plainly says, "His own self bare our sins in His own body *on the tree*" (1 Peter 2:25). Nothing short of death is the wages of sin. It is sometimes urged that Romans 5:19 teaches otherwise, "By the obedience of One shall many be made righteous." But a careful reading of the whole passage, verses 12 to 21, shows that it exactly confirms the Scripture quoted from Peter. Paul is contrasting the two Heads, Adam and Christ — the sin of the one with its attendant train of disaster; the righteousness, the obedience of the other with its attendant train of blessing. It is a question of the "one offence" and the "one righteousness" (verse 18, margin). Christ's ONE righteousness was obedience even unto His DEATH.

If the Blood cleanses us from all sin, what need is there for the water?

Let us answer that question by asking another. Are you not conscious that you as much need cleansing from the *love* of sin as from the *condemnation* of sin? There is great need for the "water." That Christians should hate sin as God hates it is a crying need everywhere.

Then as to the daily cleansing of which the laver speaks. Do we not need it in this defiling world? Is there not much about us personally that needs removing, to say nothing of the subtle influences of this world which often insensibly affect us? Every Christian with a sensitive conscience will surely agree that there is.

Is it not scriptural, then, to go to the blood for daily cleansing? It says "cleanseth" in 1 John 1:7.

Nowhere in Scripture do we find the idea of daily recurrence for cleansing to the blood of Christ. The argument based on the word "cleanseth" in 1 John 1:7 is not admissible. True, the word is in the present tense, but it is used simply to point out the inherent property of the precious blood. We so use the present tense in ordinary conversation. For instance, the other day a man brought a sack of quicklime into my yard, and deposited it in a quiet corner out of harm's way, remarking, "It will be all right there, the rain will soon settle it. Water slakes lime, you know."

What did he mean? Not that the water was going to slake that lime repeatedly, almost every day, for lime can be slaked but once; he just referred to the well-known property of water in regard to lime, a property that holds good at all times and everywhere.

It is thus the apostle speaks in 1 John 1:7.

But Scripture does speak of our repeatedly being washed in the water; and if we insist on this distinction it is not for the sake of mere theological accuracy. To teach that we must have repeated recurrence to the blood for fresh applications thereof does great harm in a twofold way. First it dishonours the blood of Christ; and second, it repeatedly puts back the saint into the place of the sinner to go through the cleansing and justifying process over and over again.

The truth is that "by *one* offering He hath perfected *for ever* them that are sanctified" (Heb. 10:14). Let us hold fast to that.

Tell us a little more about this daily cleansing by water. How do we get it?

By the Word. The water and the Word are clearly connected in such a passage as "That He might sanctify and cleanse it with the washing of water by the Word (Eph. 5:26).

The Word of God it is which brings home to our souls the death of Christ in its power and wealth of spiritual meaning. Sin in its true hideousness stands revealed, and our affections are cleansed thereby. "Wherewithal shall a young man cleanse his way? by taking heed thereto according to Thy Word" (Psa. 119:9).

We often overlook this cleansing effect of God's Word, while eager, it may be, for a better textual acquaintance with it.

A believer once lamented to an old saint of riper experience the difficulty she had in remembering the points of Christian teaching to which she listened. He bade her go with the sieve she held in her hand to the pump hard by and bring him a sieve full of water. She thought it a strange request, as by the time she reached him every drop was lost. He bade her to do it again, again and yet again. She affirmed it to be a useless task, when he explained his parable by pointing out that if not one drop of water had been retained at any rate the sieve was MUCH CLEANER *for the process*!

Let us dwell much upon the Word of God. We may never become deeply versed in Scriptural lore — that is a secondary consideration —

our lives and ways will at all events be cleansed thereby.

In John 3 we read of being born of water; is there a connection between that and what we are speaking of, or does it refer to baptism?

It links itself with that of which we are speaking. By the water of the Word applied in the power of the Holy Spirit of God we are born again — made to possess a new life and nature which carries with it the condemnation of the old. It is typified by the bathing of the priests from head to foot (*see* Exod. 29:4 and John 13:10).

It does not refer to baptism. A quiet consideration of the passage makes this manifest. Notice (1) the Lord only speaks of *one* new birth. This new birth (2) is said to be "of water and of the Spirit." The water the instrument, the Spirit the Power, and (3) it is expressly declared by the Lord to be in its nature *in*definable and completely *un*controlled by man (verse 8). Baptism is easily definable and completely controlled by man, and therefore NOT that of which this passage speaks.

Is it only when we sin that we need the water?

We *do* need it when we sin, but even apart from actual sins, being in a world of defilement we need it if we would worship, hold communion with, or serve God. Read Numbers 19, and you will find in type the water as purification from sin; then turn to Exodus 30:17–21, and in type you have water removing every earthly defilement in view of drawing near to God in the sanctuary without reference to actual sins. In the New Testament John 13 is more connected with the latter aspect than the former.

How dependent we are upon not only the Blood, but the Water!

Chapter Eighteen

GRACE AND DISCIPLESHIP

The very essence of the grace of God is that it is free and unconditional. The way of its reception — repentance and faith — is plainly laid down for us in Scripture, but though there may be *conditions* for its reception, grace itself is unhampered by any such thing. Some *men* are adepts at the art of giving with one hand and taking away with the other, of bestowing gifts so hedged about with restrictions and conditions as to be positively useless to the recipients; but this is not *God's* way.

"The free grace of God" is a common expression, rightly used, and most of us believe in it. Yet it is puzzling to many when, opening their Bibles, they light upon passages in which they are unexpectedly confronted by an "IF." For example, "IF any man will come after Me, let him deny himself, and take up his cross daily, and follow Me" (Luke 9:23).

What does it mean? Is salvation, after all, as free as we had supposed? Must we make a kind of bargain with the Master, after these terms, ere we can be enrolled as His?

Let us answer these questions by turning to Luke 14 and reading the paragraph, verses 25 to 35. The same thoughts reappear here: "IF any man come to Me, and hate not his father, and mother, and wife and children, and brethren, and sisters, yea, and his own life also, he cannot be My disciple." Those four closing words are thrice repeated (verses 26, 27, and 33). Not, mark you, "he cannot be saved," but "he cannot be My DISCIPLE."

Now of all the four, Luke's Gospel is the one which emphasizes grace. Indeed in Luke 14 the very paragraph which precedes the one referred to contains the parable of the great supper" (verses 15 to 24), which is a marvellous unfolding of the grace of God. Is it not worthy of note, then, that, having unfolded divine *grace* in such a way as to bring great multitudes about Him eager to hear, the Lord turns round upon them and tests their reality by proposing to them the terms of *discipleship*; and shall we not do well, while observing the distinction between them, to keep them together in the order in which He put them?

They may be distinguished as follows:

Grace is a special form or character of divine love. It is the shape it takes when it stoops to flow forth to the utterly undeserving, adapting itself to their need, though far transcending the need in the wealth of its full supplies.

Discipleship is the special form taken by the love that springs up responsively in the heart of a believer. It is the backward flow of divine love to its Source. To be a disciple is to be a *learner*, and not a learner only, but a *follower*; and when the grace of God grips a soul and new life begins, its first instincts are to learn of the Saviour and to follow Him.

Granting this, it is easy to see that grace is the mainspring of discipleship, and it is not without reason that they are linked together in Luke 14.

In the parable of the great supper we find the door of salvation swung widely open and the very worst invited. No demand is made upon them, no condition imposed, no bargain struck. Grace shines forth undimmed by any tarnish of that kind. But He who spoke that parable was well aware of two things.

1. That many would profess to receive grace, without being real in their profession.

2. That those who really receive it have thereby had begotten in their souls a responsive love that draws them irresistibly after the One from whom it comes; and such must understand what is needful if they are to follow Him.

Therefore it was that He followed up His declaration of grace with instruction as to discipleship, and added two short parables to show the importance of counting the cost.

"It costs too much to be a Christian," said a gloomy-looking man one day. Was he right?

Did he mean, "It costs too much to be *saved*"? Then he was totally wrong. The untold cost of salvation has fallen upon One who was able to bear it, and He, being made sin for us, has borne it all. To us it *costs* nothing.

Ah! but he used the word "Christian" in its proper sense, for it was the *disciples* who were called *Christians* first in Antioch (Acts 11:26). He meant, "It costs too much to be a disciple." Again, then, he was *wrong*. It costs to be a disciple, but it does not cost too much! The fact is, our gloomy-looking friend was not saved, he had never tasted grace, and therefore had nothing to spend. When a man goes to market with no money in his pocket everything costs too much! He was putting discipleship before grace, which is equivalent to putting demand before supply, and responsibility before the power that meets it — in everyday language, "putting the cart before the horse."

What does discipleship cost? It costs sacrifice in every direction and therefore the little parables come in here. It costs a good deal of labour in fortifying one's position, and a good deal of energy in fighting one's foes.

"Which of you intending to build a tower . . ." Have you any such intention? Certainly you have, if you propose to really follow the Lord. A tower speaks of protection; and such we need. Nothing is plainer in Scripture than that, though we are kept by the power of God, it is "*through faith*" (1 Peter 1:5). The responsibility to build up ourselves on our most holy faith rests upon *us*. Therefore "praying in the Holy Ghost" is the only attitude that becomes us, and the result is to keep ourselves "in the love of God" (*see* Jude 20, 21). With the love of God enveloping us as our tower of defence we are well fortified indeed!

"Faith" is the hand that builds. "*The* faith" — and we find it in the Word of God — is the mighty foundation on which we build. Prayer is the attitude best suited to these building operations. The love of God, *consciously known*, is our tower of defence.

But all this is the means to an end. We are well furnished defensively that we may act offensively against the foe. The trowel truly comes first, but after that the sword.

"Or what king going to make war . . ." Have you any thought of such an aggressive movement? If a disciple you *ought* to have. Notice, the king with ten thousand proposes to take the *offensive* against the king with twenty thousand. A bold movement that! Ah, but behind his back was a well fortified base of operations, his tower was built. This is ever God's way. David's tower was built in the wilderness experiences of meeting the lion and the bear, and hence Goliath has no terrors for him. Luther, "the monk that shook the world," advances with his tiny book into the hot-bed of animosity at Worms. Yes, but this was his battle cry:

> "A mighty fortress is our God,
> A bulwark never failing."

Discipleship means all this. It means prayer, and the study of God's Word. It means exercises otherwise unknown, and the shock of battle with the world, the flesh, and the devil. Sit down and count the cost. Do you tremble? Then recount the cost in the full light of the power of God and the weighty stores of *grace*, and you will begin to "rejoice in Christ Jesus," and yet more deeply have "no confidence in the flesh."

Thus grace and discipleship go hand-in-hand. Just how, the case of Bartimæus well illustrates (Mark 10:46–52). Grace stood still at his cry and gave him all he desired freely. "Jesus said unto him, *Go thy way*." Then, Bartimæus, no terms are imposed upon you; go north, south, east, or west, as you desire. You are free! Which way did he go? "Immediately he received his sight and followed Jesus in the way." Impelled by grace he entered the path of discipleship. *He followed Jesus.*

Is every Christian a disciple, or is it only certain ones that have this distinction?

There are no "favoured ones" in Christianity. True it is that the world having invaded and conquered the Christian profession, clergy and laity in numerous grades, corresponding to worldly society, are found on every hand. The Christianity of the Bible, while admitting spiritual gifts and office, knows nothing of these things. The early Christians were believers, saints, disciples, all of them (*see* Acts 1:15; 6:1; 9:38; 19:9; 20:7). And the very foremost of the apostles was just a believer, a saint, or a disciple along with the rest, though gifted from heaven and clothed with an authority that was indisputable.

We may be sure, therefore, that it is a fatal mistake to consider that discipleship belongs only to a few — a kind of clergy — and that we more ordinary folk may rest content with being saved, and getting to heaven presently, and need bestir ourselves as to nothing else. Shame on us if like Bartimæus we receive our sight, and then, unlike him, go strolling off to amuse ourselves with the novel sights of Jericho!

Yet there is a tendency in that direction, and therefore it was that the Lord said to certain Jews who believed on Him, "If ye continue in My Word, then are ye My disciples indeed" (John 8:31).

Discipleship does truly belong to *all* Christians, yet many believers there are who are not "DISCIPLES INDEED."

Can you summarize for us the condition of Christian discipleship?

Read carefully Luke 9, verses 23 to 26 and 46 to 62, also chapter 14, verses 25 to 33 again, if you would gain some idea of them.

The gist of it all seems to be contained in 14:26 and 33, where we find the one absolutely indispensable condition to be that Christ must be *first* and the rest — relations, possessions, and particularly one's self — *nowhere.*

We "hate . . ." not absolutely, but in a comparative sense, of course. Our love to Christ should so transcend the natural love we bear to our relations that the latter appears as hate when compared with the former. (Luke 9:59,60 gives an illustrative case).

We "forsake . . ." *i.e.*, the affections are severed from our possessions; they are no longer ours, but our Master's, to be held for Him. It *may* mean parting with everything, as in the case of the early Christians, or, like Levi, we may *leave all* and yet still have. Levi's house was still "his own," and his money was used to make a great feast for Christ and draw sinners to Him (Luke 5:27–29). A very good example for some of us!

But if Christ is to be first, self must go, and so we find that the disciple has to deny himself and to take up his cross daily.

"Deny himself," *i.e.*, say NO to self. Accept death — be as a dead man — as far as the working of will is concerned. An inward thing.

"Take up his cross daily," *i.e.*, an outward thing. Accept death as cutting off from the world and its glory. Say NO to the love of reputation and popularity.

Stern work this. Bitter to the flesh. Sweetened by the love of Christ. These are the conditions of discipleship.

It is easy to see what discipleship meant for the early Christians. We live in different days. What does it means practically for us to-day?

It means precisely the same now as then. The only difference is one of surface details. It means saying *no* to our own wills as much as ever. It means the cross — disallowance by the world — as much as ever. The world disallowed them by cross or sword, by wild beast or flame; it may disallow us by silent contempt, a well-timed snub, or social ostracism. The thing is the same; but in their case an *acute* attack, short, sharp, and all was over; in ours, *chronic*, not severe, but lingering and protracted.

It means walking in the spirit of self-judgment, and separation from the world, even in its religious forms. It means giving up many things lawful in themselves for the sake of His name. It means making THE question at all times and under all circumstances, not "What do I want?" but "What does He want?"

It looks then as if the true disciple stands to lose a good deal in this world. What does he gain?

He gains "manifold more in this present time, and in the world to come life everlasting" (Luke 18:30). The profit will not be of the nature that appeals to the man of the world, who estimates chiefly by the amount of his balance at the bank. It is more real than that. Here are words which indicate its character: "If any man serve Me, let him follow Me; and where I am, there shall also My servant be: if any man serve Me, him will My Father honour" (John 12:26).

Companionship with Christ; honour from the Father. Who can estimate the gain of those two things? A glimpse of them was granted to the three disciples, when, having been plainly told what discipleship would involve, they witnessed the transfiguration (Luke 9) — when they were "with Him in the holy mount" (2 Peter 1:16–18).

Small wonder, then, that Paul — who stood in the front rank of disciples and suffered the loss of all things for Christ — when he fixed the eye of faith on eternal things dismissed the *loss* side of the *discipleship* account as, "our light affliction," and hailed the profit side as "*a far more exceeding and eternal weight of glory*" (2 Cor. 4:17,18).

Is there any difference between a disciple and an apostle? If so, what?

There is a very distinct difference. We read, "He called unto Him His disciples: and of them He chose twelve whom also He named apostles" (Luke 6:13). The word "disciple" means "one taught" or "trained." The word "apostle" means "one sent forth." Every true follower of the Lord was a disciple; only the twelve were sent forth by Him as apostles. Theirs was a peculiar place, therefore, of authority and service.

Moreover, the apostles had to do with the foundations of the Church (Eph. 2:20), and have long since passed away; but ever since then and unto this day disciples of Christ are to be found on earth.

Where does the power for discipleship come from, and how can we keep it up?

The necessary power is not to be found within yourself, nor can it be worked up by religious exercises. It is in God alone. It reaches us, however, in a very simple way. Dr. Chalmers it was, who spoke of "the *ex*pulsive power of a new affection." We may just as truly speak of "the *im*pulsive power of a new affection." Let the bright rays of the love of God break into any heart, however dark, and straightway a new impelling power is known and discipleship begins.

That which *starts* it *sustains* it. Read John, chapters 14–16. They are a perfect manual of discipleship. You will find that *love* is the spring of everything. The Comforter, the *Holy Spirit*, is the power, and *obedience*, the keeping and the doing of Christ's commandments, is the pathway into which the disciple's feet are led.

> Can you give us any hints to help us, as we seek to
> live as disciples of the Lord Jesus?

I should just say three things:

1. You will need wisdom and discretion. Therefore you must give the Scriptures their proper place. The will of our Master and Lord is therein expressed; our business as disciples is to search out that will in dependence on the Holy Spirit's teaching. The Scriptures must therefore be to us the Word of God, and we must make them our careful study.

2. You must maintain a spirit of dependence upon God. Therefore prayer is necessary. The disciple must needs ever cultivate the prayerful spirit.

3. You must ever seek the pathway of obedience. As disciples our great business is to obey rather than to do the greatest of exploits. Prince Rupert, of historic fame, performed great exploits in the service of Charles the First. But his exploits in large measure contributed to the smashing defeat which Charles suffered at the hand of Cromwell's Ironsides at Naseby, and led to the loss not only of his master's crown, but his head also. If he had thought less of his individual exploits and more of the leader's plan of campaign, results might have been different.

Obedience to God's Word is our first business. Let us lay aside every weight that would hinder us, remembering the words of the great Master Himself: "If ye know these things, happy are ye if ye do them" (John 13:17).

Chapter Nineteen

ELECTION
AND
FREE GRACE

From the beginning of Scripture history, two great facts, forming the basis of all God's dealings with men, have been apparent. First, God is absolutely sovereign. Second, man is an intelligent creature with moral faculties and responsible to his Creator.

But these two facts, the sovereignty of God on the one hand, the responsibility of man on the other, have always presented a difficulty to certain minds, particularly when it is a question of the practical work of preaching the Gospel, and of the reception of it by the sinner. Between the sovereignty of God expressing itself in the election of some for blessing, and the free offer of grace that addresses itself to all, there seems to be some contradiction which it is difficult to avoid, some discrepancy not easily explained.

Of course, if we are at liberty to discard one of these facts in favour of the other, and throw ourselves into the arms of either a hard hyper-Calvinism, or a weak Arminianism, as the case may be, the difficulty may vanish. But this would mean the sacrifice of truth. Since we are not at liberty to do this, but have to accept both these facts (for both plainly lie on the surface of Scripture), we must humbly seek the divine solution, assured that the only real difficulty is the littleness of our minds, and of their ability to grasp the thoughts of God.

We have but to open our Bibles at the beginning to find both these truths. "In the beginning God created the heaven and the earth" (Gen. 1:1). Here is declared the one truth. "Let us make man in our image, after our likeness: and let them have dominion" (Gen. 1:26). Here is declared the other. Man was made in God's image, *i.e.*, as God's representative in creation. He was after God's likeness, inasmuch as he was originally a free, intelligent, moral agent. And though no longer sinless but fallen, his responsibility remains.

It would be difficult to find a finer confession of the sovereignty of God than that made by Nebuchadnezzar, the great Gentile monarch in whom *human* sovereignty reached its highest expression. He said, "He doeth according to His will in the army of heaven, and among the inhabitants of the earth: and none can stay His hand, or say unto Him, What doest Thou?" (Dan. 4:35).

Nor can we point to a more striking unfolding of the responsibility of man in his fallen estate than that given by Paul in his powerful argument (Rom. 1:18 to 3:19) to prove the complete ruin of the race. If sin and degradation destroyed a man's responsibility there would be every excuse for his condition, but the most degraded heathen is shown to be "without excuse," as is also the polished idolater and the religious Jew.

Thus far all seems plain. The difficulty occurs when we begin to *apply* these truths. Believers are addressed as "chosen in Him before the foundation of the world" (Eph. 1:4), as "elect according to the foreknowledge of God the Father" (1 Peter 1:2). To His disciples the Lord Jesus distinctly said, "Ye have not chosen Me, but I have chosen you" (John 15:16); and again, "No man can come to Me, except the Father which hath sent Me draw him" (John 6:44). Shall we reason from these scriptures that since the choice is God's and no one comes to Christ unless drawn of the Father, therefore all effort in connection with the Gospel is useless; that, in fact, to preach to any except those chosen of God is waste of time?

On the other hand, Peter urged his hearers, when pricked in their heart, "Save yourselves from this untoward generation" (Acts 2:40). To careless and rebellious sinners he said, "Repent ye therefore, and be converted" (Acts 3:19). Paul tells us that he testified to both Jews and Greeks "repentance toward God and faith toward our Lord Jesus Christ" (Acts 20:21).

Shall we disregard these apostolic utterances? Ought they rather to have run something after this fashion: "Men and brethren, you can do absolutely nothing. You are spiritually dead and therefore you must simply wait the pleasure of God. If He has elected you, you will be saved. If not, you will be lost"? Or shall we adopt the opposite view, and do our best to explain away these reference's to God's sovereign work in connection with conversion, saying that they only mean that God, being omniscient, knows the end from the beginning, that He has no particular will as regards anybody, that man is an absolutely free agent, quite capable of choosing the right if put before him in a sufficiently attractive way, and that therefore we ought to do everything possible to make the Gospel palatable and win men?

To incline to either set of scriptures at the expense of the other would be, indeed, to expose ourselves to the keen edge of those searching words, "O fools, and slow of heart to believe *all* that the prophets have spoken" (Luke 24:25).

Any difficulties we may have as to these things would, we believe, largely vanish if we better undersood the true character of *the ruin of man* and *the grace of God*.

In what does the ruin of man consist? By sinning he has placed himself under a burden of guilt and has rendered himself liable to judgment. There is more than this, however. He has also become possessed of a fallen nature utterly and incorrigibly bad, with a heart "deceitful above all things, and desperately wicked" (Jer. 17:9). But even this is not all. Sin has acted like a subtle poison in his veins and has so stupefied and perverted his reason, will and judgment, that "there is none that understandeth, there is none that seeketh after God" (Rom. 3:11). Even in the presence of grace and the sweet pleadings of the Gospel men reject the Saviour provided, and with perverse unanimity prefer the empty follies of the world. Like the "great herd of swine" they rush madly to destruction, and hence the only hope is a sovereign interposition of God.

The parable of the "great supper" (Luke 14) illustrates this. The well-laden suppertable represents the spiritual blessings resulting from the death of Christ. At great cost all is ready, and yet all seems to have been provided in vain. Something else is needed: *the mission of the Holy Spirit*, pictured by the errand of "the servant." Things were brought to a successful issue, and the house was filled, only because of His "compelling" operations.

If we once realize the full extent of that ruin into which sin has plunged us, we shall be delivered from the "Arminian" extreme, and shall recognize that the sovereign action of God in choosing us and drawing us by the compelling power of His Spirit was our only hope. Instead of quarrelling with this side of the truth, it will bow our hearts in grateful worship before Him.

Poor fallen, self-destroyed man is still, however, a responsible creature. Reason, will, and judgment may be perverted, but they are not destroyed. Hence the largeness of the grace of God.

What is grace? Is it the particular goodness which visits and saves the souls of the elect? No. That is *mercy*. In Romans 9 and 11, where election is the great subject, mercy is mentioned again and again. *Grace* is the mighty outflow of the heart of God towards the utterly sinful and undeserving. It shows no partiality. It knows no restrictions. It is a wide and deep sea. "All men" (1 Tim. 2:3–6) are its only boundaries, and "where sin abounded, grace did much more abound" (Rom. 5:20) is the only measure of its depth.

We hear the accents of grace in the last great commission of the risen Christ to His disciples, "that repentance and remission of sins should be preached in His name among all nations, beginning at Jerusalem" (Luke 24:47). How akin were these instructions to those given by the King in that other parable of a feast, recorded in Matthew 22: "Go ye therefore into the highways, and as many as ye shall find, bid to the marriage." In this parable we have not "the servant," as in Luke, but "the servants." It is not the Spirit of God in His sovereign and secret activities, but saved men who, without knowing aught of these secret things, simply do the King's business. Do they find anyone in the broad highways of the world? Then without raising questions as to their character, or as to whether chosen or not, they give the invitation. All who listen are gathered in, both bad and good: and the wedding is "furnished with guests."

Is there any great difficulty in this? Surely not. Knowing that it pleases God "by the foolishness of preaching to save them that believe," the evangelist proclaims the glad tidings far and wide. When men believe his message, he attributes that work to the Spirit of God, and rejoices over them, knowing their election of God (1 Thess. 1:4).

Nor is there anything to stumble the seeking sinner. The very fact that he is seeking indicates that he is being drawn of the Father. The idea that a sinner may be even in an agony of seeking for the Saviour in this day of grace, and yet be unheard because not elected, is a hideous distortion of truth. The words of the Lord Jesus are as true as ever: "Seek and ye shall find" (Matt. 7:7).

The fact is, election has nothing to do with the sinner as such. No hint of it is breathed in any recorded preaching of the apostles, though it is frequently mentioned, to establish the faith of believers. As a rule, it is only when unbalanced preachers of extreme views take it from its setting in Scripture and thrust it upon their unconverted hearers that it creates difficulty in their minds.

Can it be shown that "election" does really mean anything more than that God knows everything, and therefore knows from the beginning who will believe and who will not?

Most assuredly. In 1 Peter 1:2 we read, "Elect according to the foreknowledge of God the Father." Election, then, is distinct from foreknowledge, though based upon it. God's election or choice is not a blind, fatalistic casting of the lot. That is a purely heathen conception. There is some such legend in connection with Buddha. When men were created it is said that he cast a lot, saying, "These to heaven, and I care not; these to hell and I care not." But our God and Father does not act like this. He choses in the full light of His foreknowledge. Hence no sinner, who ever really wants to be saved, finds the door shut against him because he is not one of the elect. His very desire is the fruit of the Spirit's work. And God's choice, as in the case of Esau and Jacob, is always justified by results. (Compare Rom. 9:12,13 with Mal. 1:2,3).

If God must elect at all, why did He not elect everybody?

How can I tell you that? Is it likely that God will tell us, who are but His creatures, the motives that underlie His decrees? If He did explain, would our finite minds be able to grasp the explanation? We may rest assured that all His decrees are in perfect harmony with the fact that "God is light" and "God is love." For the rest, if any man be contentious we content ourselves with quoting the inspired words: "Behold . . . I will answer thee, God is greater than man. Why dost thou strive against Him? for *He giveth not account of any of His matters*" (Job 33:12,13). After all, being God, why should He?

If man be morally incapable of going or choosing right, how can he be really responsible?

Let me answer by an analogy. If, in the case of that poor creature making her 201st appearance before the magistrates on the old charge, "drunk and disorderly," the plea were raised that since she was so degraded as to be morally incapable of resisting alcohol or choosing a better life, she was no longer responsible, or amenable to punishment, would it avail? Of course not. No sane person imagines that one has only to sink low enough into crime to be absolved from responsibility.

Alas! who can measure the depths of perversity and incapacity into which man has plunged himself by sin? Nevertheless his responsibility remains.

Does "free grace" mean that salvation is ours simply by a choice which lies in the exercise of our own free will?

It does not. It means that as far as the *intentions* of God's Gospel are concerned, all are embraced. Christ died for all (1 Tim. 2:4,6). To all the Gospel is sent, just as freely as if it were certain that all would as naturally receive it, as, alas! they naturally reject it. Multitudes, however, *do* receive it, and then the righteousness of God which is "unto all" in its intention is "upon all them that believe" in its actual effect (Rom. 3:22–24. Such are saved by grace, through faith, and that not of themselves, it is the gift of God (Eph. 2:8). Their blessing is of God from first to last, and they are entitled to regard themselves as chosen of Him.

Has the sinner to choose Christ?

If we wish to speak with scriptural accuracy, the answer must be, No. He has to *receive* Christ; but that is a somewhat different matter. *Choose* is a word with active force. It implies certain powers of discrimination and selection. To speak of a sinner choosing Christ supposes that he has powers which he does not possess.

Receive is passive rather than active in force. It implies that instead of exercising his powers, the sinner simply falls into line with God's offer. It is the word Scripture uses.

The children of God are said to be "as many as *received*" Christ (John 1:12), and this receiving was the result not of their free-will, but of God's gracious operation; they were "born . . . of God" (verse 13).

Are we right in urging sinners to repent and believe?

Certainly. Our blessed Lord Himself did so (Mark 1:15). So did Peter (Acts 3:19), and Paul (Acts 16:31; 20:21; 26:20). We have not only to proclaim that faith is the principle on which God justifies the sinner, but we have to *urge* men to believe. The fact that faith is the result of God's work in the soul and that all spiritual enlargement for the believer is through the operation of God's Spirit, in no way militates against the servant of God being much in earnest and persuading men.

Paul preached at Thessalonica "with much contention" (1 Thess. 2:2) — "with much earnest striving" the New Translation renders it. He speaks of *persuading* men" (2 Cor. 5:11), and with Barnabas he *persuaded* certain converts "to continue in the grace of God" (Acts 13:43).

These examples are enough to outweigh any amount of reasoning to the contrary.

How would you answer a person who says, "I can't believe until God gives me the power"?

I would remark that both repentance and faith are things which do not require power so much as weakness. To repent, is to own the truth as to yourself; to believe, is to lean your poor shattered soul on Christ.

Again I would point out that God's command is man's enabling. The man with a withered hand is a case in point (Luke 6:6–10). The power was there instantly the word was spoken.

Does a sinner wish to insinuate that he is very anxious to believe, but that God will not give him ability to do so because of certain fatalistic decrees? Tell him plainly it is not true. He is leaving sober fact for the nightmare of fallen reason. Never does the smallest bit of desire toward Christ spring up in a sinner's heart but there is a grace to bring it to fruition in definite faith. Probably the questioner would prove to be a trifler bent on quibbling, in which case we should have to leave him. A really perplexed and anxious soul I would urge (instead of occupying himself about questions as to God's sovereignty, which are, and must be, above the ken of finite man) to rest with simple confidence in the Saviour, and to give heed to those great verities, which are so plainly declared that "the way-faring men, though fools, shall not err therein."

"Never let what you do not know disturb what you do know," said a wise and good man.

Never forget that He who said, "All that the Father giveth Me shall come to Me," immediately added: "and him that cometh to Me I will in no wise cast out" (John 6:37).

Chapter Twenty

———————

ISRAEL
AND
THE CHURCH

A knowledge of "dispensational truth," as it is often termed, is indispensable for the intelligent reading of the Bible. Yet many Christians seem to have hardly given it a thought.

God has been pleased to deal with men at different times in various ways. Fresh revelations of Himself and of His will have ushered in new modes of dealing with men, new *dispensations*.

"Dispensational truth" teaches us to rightly distinguish these changes, and to discern their nature, so that the salient features of each may not be obscured. The importance of this for us Christians is that we thereby learn the true character of the calling wherewith we are called from on high, and of the age in which our lot is cast.

Up to the time of Christ a dispensation ran its course in which the prominent feature was Israel, the chosen nation of the stock of Abraham. The period in which we live, from Pentecost to the coming of the Lord, is marked by altogether different features. Not Israel, but the Church is prominent in God's thoughts to-day.

Before dwelling on the important distinctions between the two, let us be quite sure that we understand exactly what we are speaking about.

By ISRAEL we do not mean the Jews, the scattered nation as they are to-day, nor as they were in the time of our Lord, a remnant still clinging to their ancient capital, Jerusalem. We do not allude to them as they actually existed at any time, but rather to what that nation was *according to God's original plan for them*.

When we speak of THE CHURCH we do not refer to any ecclesiastical building nor to any denomination, nor to any number of professed

Christians banded together into what is called nowadays "a church." We use the term in its scriptural sense. The Greek word rendered "church" simply means "called-out ones." Those, who are called out of the world by God during this period of Christ's rejection, are by this means, and by the indwelling of the Holy Ghost, banded together into God's assembly, the church.

It may be helpful to notice that in Scripture the term "church" is used in three ways: —

1. As denoting the aggregate number of the Christians in any given place (1 Cor. 1:2; Col. 4:15, etc.).

2. As the aggregate number of all Christians upon earth at any given time (1 Cor. 10:32; 12:28; Eph. 1:22, etc.). In this aspect the church is like a regiment which abides the same, though the units which compose it are constantly changing.

3. As the aggregate number of all Christians, called out and sealed with the Spirit between Pentecost and the coming of the Lord (Eph. 3:21; 5:25, etc.).

Of these the last is the sense in which we use the word here; though, if we speak of the church as it exists on earth to-day, we obviously allude to it in its second aspect.

Be it remembered, however, that we refer, as in the case of Israel, not to what the church actually is, or has at any time been, but to what it is according to the original design and thought of God.

Having defined our terms, let us observe a few necessary distinctions.

1. John, the forerunner of the Lord, was the last of the long line of the prophets of the past dispensation. With him, God's utterances under the old covenant reached their full stop. With Christ, the new utterances began. "The law and the prophets were until John; since that time the kingdom of God is preached" (Luke 16:16).

The advent of Christ into the world was described by Zacharias as the coming of the dayspring (or, as the margin reads, "sunrising") from on high. His appearance on earth heralded the dawn of a new day. Not that this new day was there and then inaugurated. The Lord Jesus had a mission to fulfil in the midst of Israel, and He must needs present Himself to that nation as their long-promised Messiah. Moreover, the broad foundations of purposed blessing must be laid amid the sufferings of Calvary. But when all this was past, when the Son of God had died and risen again, when He had ascended to heaven and sent down the Holy Ghost, then was inaugurated a dispensation that was new indeed, utterly different from all that had gone before.

2. The characteristic feature of the old dispensation was *law*, that of the new is *grace*. The giving of the law at Sinai ushered in the former. God formulated His demands upon men. He was to receive, and they were to give, that which was His due. The fact that failure came in immediately, failure so great as to amount to a total collapse, did not relieve men of their newly incurred responsibilities in the smallest degree. God, however, announced to Moses that He would have mercy (Exod. 33:19), and withhold the threatened destruction in view of the coming of Christ. The law still held sway as "schoolmaster," and continued so to do until Christ came (Gal. 3:24).

In Christ a power mightier than the law was present. The case of the sinful woman in John 8 beautifully illustrates it. Under the potent influence of grace, the hypocrites were convicted far more effectually than under law, and the sinner was forgiven, a thing which the law never professed to do. Now God *gives* and man *receives*. The new dispensation is marked by *grace* reigning through righteousness, unto eternal life, by Jesus Christ our Lord (Rom. 5:21).

3. The old dispensation centred round Israel, the new is connected with the church.

The law was given not to everybody, but to one nation, Israel. Upon that *nation*, therefore, God's attention was focussed. The privileges of the children of Israel belonged to them nationally rather than individually. God always had His own secret dealings with the souls of individuals, and these dealings came into greater prominence in the days of national apostasy. But at the beginning God took them up nationally without reference to the spiritual state of individuals, and their standing before Him was on a national basis.

On the other hand, there is nothing national about the church. Peter declared, corroborated by James, that the divine programme for this dispensation is the visiting of the nations by God, "to take out of them a people for His name" (Acts 15:13,14). God is now making an election from all nations, and those thus gathered out for His name compose "the church."

The church, then, is not national, nor is it international, it is rather extra-national, *i.e.*, altogether outside of all national distinctions, and totally independent of them. Instead of being constructed on a national basis, it is represented in Scripture as "one flock" (John 10:16, R.V.), as "one body" (1 Cor. 12:13), as "a spiritual house, an holy priesthood" (1 Peter 2:5), as a family composed of the children of God (1 John 2:12; 3:1, etc.).

Moreover, in connection with the church God begins with the individual. It is composed of those who have personally been set in right relations with God. Only as forgiven, and as having received the Spirit to indwell them, do they become members of the one body, and "living stones" in the spiritual house.

4. Connected with Israel was a ritualistic worship, the value of which lay in its typical significance. The church's privileges are connected with the eternal realities themselves, with the substance rather than with the shadows. Her worship does not consist of sacrificial offerings, symbolic ceremonies, and the like, but is "worship in spirit and in truth."

The law had only "a shadow of good things to come, and not the very image of the things" (Heb. 10:1). The good things have come, and are realized by Christians today. Christ has established them (Heb. 9:24; 10:12), the Spirit has revealed them (1 Cor. 2:9,10), and the believer may gaze upon them with the eye of faith (2 Cor. 4:18).

5. Israel's blessings and privileges were largely of an earthly and material order, the church's are heavenly and spiritual.

In the Old Testament instructions were given as to the way in which the children of Israel should return thanks to God when they were actually in possession of the promised land. They were to take the first of all their fruits and set them in a basket before the Lord their God, with an acknowledgment of His goodness on their lips (Deut. 26:1–11).

Is the Christian to approach God in this way? On the contrary, when Paul wrote to the Ephesians as to the heavenly inheritance of Christians, far from speaking of material things, he said, "Blessed be the God and Father of our Lord Jesus Christ, who hath blessed us with all *spiritual* blessings in *heavenly* places in Christ" (Eph. 1:3).

How complete the contrast!

6. While Israel's destiny is to be the channel of blessing to all nations, during the golden years of the millennial age, the church's destiny is association with Christ in heaven. Isaiah 60 well describes the future of Israel. Revelation 19 and 21, under various figures, present to us the destiny of the church as "the Lamb's wife."

Was there a definite time when God's ways with Israel ended and when the church period began?

It has already been pointed out that the death of Christ marked the close of God's dealings with Israel as a nation; and that His resurrection and the descent of the Holy Spirit on the day of Pentecost inaugurated the present dispensation. Compare Acts 2:41–47 with 1 Corinthians 12:13.

Two qualifying remarks must, however, be made.

Firstly, that though God's ways with Israel reached their great climax in the cross, He, nevertheless, continued certain supplementary dealings with them until the death of Stephen, and perhaps even until the destruction of Jerusalem. Nor were the full designs of God as to the church made known in their entirety at the very outset of the present age. They were gradually revealed through the apostles, particularly through Paul, though the church itself began its corporate existence as stated.

Secondly, that God's ways with Irsael have only ended *for a time*. Later on, in a day still future, they will be resumed, and the glorious promises made to that favoured nation be literally fulfilled. Israel has been side-tracked, as it were, while the church occupies the rails. When the church has been transferred to heaven, Israel will again be brought out upon the main line of God's dealings.

In Acts 7:38 Stephen speaks of "the church in the wilderness." And the headings to many Old Testament chapters refer to the church. Does it not appear from this that the church was in existence before Christ came.

Israel was undoubtedly "the assembly in the wilderness." Is there anything in this which would warrant our identifying Israel with the church of the New Testament? No more than the use of the same word in Acts 19:41 warrants our confounding the church in that city with the unruly mob of Diana's worshippers.

The application to the church of prophetic utterances in Old Testament headings of chapters (which are no part of the original text) is due to the mistaken views of well-meaning men.

But the mistake is a serious one, because it is by the confusion of Israel with the church that men have sought to justify the introduction into Christianity of Jewish elements and principles.

Were not such men as Abraham, Moses, and Elijah in the church? Does it not put a slight upon these honoured men to deny them a place therein?

By no means. Their lot was cast in the dispensation that is past. Viewed *morally*, these men tower as giants, while many of us Christians are but pigmies. Yet even John the Baptist, than whom none was greater, was, when viewed dispensationally, less then the least in the kingdom of heaven (Matt. 11:11). He belonged to the age of servitude, we to the age of sonship (*see* Gal. 4:1–7).

The Lord's words in Matthew 11 concerning John were followed by those of Matthew 16:13–18 concerning Himself. He was not a mere prophet like Elijah, Jeremiah, or John, but the Son of the living God, and on that rock, said He, "I will build My church." Mark those two words: "*will build.*" It was a future work of which the Lord spoke, and one in which these great men of old had no part.

What was God's object in calling out Israel into the special place they occupied?

They were called to take possession of the promised land for God, as a kind of pledge that the whole earth belonged to Him, in spite of the fact that Satan had usurped dominion over it. When they entered they crossed the Jordan as the people of "*the Lord of all the earth*" (Josh.

3:11,13).

Further, they were to preserve in the world the stock "of whom as concerning the flesh Christ came" (Rom. 9:5).

Incidentally also, in that nation as a sample separated from the corruptions of the surrounding peoples, and privileged beyond all others, was made God's last trial of the human race. The records of their own law as cited in Romans 3:9–18 testified to their irremediable failure, and proved in this way the hopelessly fallen conditions of all. If, as Romans 3:19 puts it, the law utterly condemns the sample nation of the Jews, who were under it, then *every* mouth is stopped, and *all the world* is "guilty before God."

What is God's object and purpose in connection with the church?

The church is Christ's body (Eph.1:23). Therefore in it He is to be expressed; just as your body is that in which *you* live and express yourself.

It represents Him here during the time of His rejection and personal absence in heaven. Satan has got rid of Christ personally from the earth, but He is here as represented in His people. To touch the church, or any who belong to it, is to touch Him. Do not His own words to Saul imply this: "Saul, Saul, why persecutest thou Me?" (Acts 9:4).

It is God's house, the only house He has upon earth at the present time. God will not be turned out of His own world! He dwells, therefore, to-day in a house which no Nebuchadnezzar, no Titus can burn to the ground, and which no Nero, no Torquemada has been able to destroy.

God's ultimate purpose is to have a bride for Christ (Eph. 5:25–27), a people who, sharing now as heavenly strangers His rejection, find their eternal portion as sharers of His heavenly glory.

Can you enumerate some of the blessings we Christians have, which even the best in Israel had not before Christ came?

The knowledge of God as Father, fully revealed in Christ, is one of the greatest of these blessings. "No man hath seen God at any time; the only begotten Son which is in the bosom of the Father, He hath declared Him" (John1:18).

Another blessing is, instead of *promises*, we have the *fact* of accomplished redemption. The promissory bank-note has been exchanged for the fine gold of the finished work of Christ.

Further, the Holy Spirit now *indwells* believers (*see* John 14:16; Acts 2:1–4). Though He had always exerted His influence upon earth, His abiding presence here is a new thing.

Lastly, our relationships with God are on an entirely new footing in Christ. We are no more servants, but sons (Gal. 4:4–6).

Much more might be added, but these four facts will serve to show the wealth of blessing that belongs to the Christian.

Shall we not thank God that our lot is cast *on this side of the cross of Christ*?

Chapter Twenty-one

WORSHIP AND
SERVICE

Christianity in its practical out-workings is a well-balanced combination of the passive and active sides of divine life in the soul. Every Christian is of necessity a receiver, not only at conversion, but all through his career. He must daily sit at Jesus' feet and hear His Word (Luke 10:39), cultivating that quiet passivity of soul which ensures a receptive state. Otherwise he has nothing to impart.

On the other hand, having received, he finds himself constrained to give. Is he rejoicing in the knowledge of sins forgiven? His joy will not be complete until he has told the news to some one else. Has some fresh truth of Scripture burst upon his view? It will not be fully his until he has acted upon it. To practise any truth is to possess that truth indeed.

So the two things go hand in hand. A Christian resembles a reservoir, inasmuch as he must have an inlet and an outflow. If he becomes so enamoured of the activities of Christianity that he is always attempting to give out without stopping to take in, spiritual emptiness and bankruptcy are the result. If he degenerates into a dreamy mystic, decrying all forms of Christian activity under cover of zeal for larger reception of divine truth, spiritual surfeit will supervene, and his ultimate loss will be great.

"From him that hath not shall be taken away even that which he hath" (Matt. 25:29). This was said of the servant who *received* a talent, but did not *give* it out to usury.

"For we must share if we would keep
That good thing from above;
Ceasing to give, we cease to have,
Such is the law of love."

All activities of a distinctly Christian character flow from one source: LOVE, the love of God known and produced in the soul. They range themselves under two heads. First, there are those activities which have God alone for their object and end. Second, those which, though God's glory is their end, have man in some way as their immediate object. Let us briefly consider these two things.

WORSHIP must stand first. It is a spiritual activity which, having God alone as its object, confers no tangible benefit upon any one in the world. Therefore, in this utilitarian age it is greatly neglected, and its true character little understood. Let Christians, be they few or many, assemble together, drawing consciously into the presence of God and pouring out their hearts in thanksgiving and worship, and there will be not a few ready to rebuke them and say, "Why was this waste of the ointment made?" They will be told to go out and do something that will confer a practical benefit upon somebody, and abandon that which does nobody any good.

But things have gone even further than this. There are many professed ministers of Christ who so fully "mind earthly things" (Phil. 3:19) that they have no thought for "the things which are above" (Col. 3:1), which the believer is bidden to seek. Their aim is limited to the benefit of men, and that in the most material way. Mark the pitiful spiritual degradation to which they have sunk as witnessed by their activities. Here is a flagrant example.

"By training people in music, developing orators and athletes, starting 'Bible classes — with heaps of fun,' and making the church a social centre, the writer has created a new community spirit, and as a result land-values are going up."

Thus an article in an American magazine described how a church may be "run" so as to benefit the whole community.

Such activities are neither worship nor service. There is nothing in them for God, and nothing for the spiritual benefit of man. Such "ministers" and "churches" must have long ago practically banished the word *worship* from their vocabularies; the idea which the word properly conveys they probably never had.

What, then, is worship? In the Old Testament the term frequently occurs and is often used in a purely ceremonial sense. The Hebrew word most frequently used means literally "to bow oneself down." In the New Testament the word gets the inward and spiritual meaning with which we are concerned, and signifies the up-flow of responsive love, in adoration, from the believer to God, now known as Father.

In John 4 the Lord Jesus, speaking to the woman of Samaria, carefully distinguishes between the "true worshippers" and the worshippers according to the ancient rites, whether at Jerusalem or Samaria, and instructs us as to the essentials for true worship. After speaking of *the Father* as the object of worship, He adds: "God is a Spirit; and they that worship Him must worship Him in spirit and in truth."

Do not these words plainly show that it is God *as Father* that we are to worship? and, further, that He is only to be worshipped according to what He has revealed Himself to be?

"*In spirit*," for "Spirit" is what God Himself is. True worship, then, is not a matter of religious emotions roused by impressive ritual or sensuous music. "Spirit" is the highest part of man, and unless we worship in spirit we do not worship at all.

"*In truth*." What is truth? We may answer Pilate's famous question thus: The realities of God Himself, that which God has revealed Himself to be: this is truth. The One who stood, crowned with thorns that day, in the judgment hall was Himself the truth, though Pilate knew it not, nor cared to know. He, and He alone, could say: "I am ... the Truth" (John 14:6), for He alone is the perfect revelation of God, and it is as Father that He has revealed Him. Therefore He said: "He that hath seen Me hath seen *the Father*" (John 14:9).

The Father, then, is to be worshipped "in truth," in the light of that revelation which has come to us in Christ. That which does not give Christ His right place is no true worship. Worshipping God and rejoicing in Christ Jesus go hand in hand (Phil. 3:3).

All this is of great importance. Let the soul firmly grasp the fact that true worship is "in spirit" and it will be delivered from the ritualistic idea which supposes that God can be worshipped by men's hands, that the more imposing the ceremony, the more gorgeous the surroundings, the more acceptable the "worship" is.

On the other hand, to know that only worship "in truth" is acceptable to God is to have the rationalistic idea dispelled. Neither the torchlight of science nor the study of God's handiwork in nature gives rise to worship. The knowledge of God Himself, revealed in Christ, is essential.

After worship comes SERVICE, the outcome of the gracious activity of divine love in the hearts of believers, leading them to an endless variety of labour for the glory of God and the good of souls.

Let us make no mistake here. The very essence of true service is that, while undertaken that others may be benefited, it is done *for the pleasure and under the direction of the Lord Jesus Christ.*

In service our one motive should be to please the Lord, who has in this Himself become our great Example. Speaking of the Father, He said: "I do always those things that please Him" (John 8:29). To do right things is not enough. Right things done with a wrong motive are wrong in the sight of heaven.

Neither is it enough to act even with a right motive, if we are acting simply on our own initiative and doing what seems right in our own eyes. A man employed in a workshop may be a good workman, but a poor servant. If he is opinionated and independent, he will be continually running counter to his master's wishes and will give no end of trouble. Again, the Lord Jesus comes before us as our Example, saying: "My meat is to do the will of Him that sent Me, and to finish His work" (John 4:34). Service, then, is not merely work, not even good work, Christian activity of the most scriptural sort, but rather such activity under the direction of the Lord.

If an illustration of our theme be wanted, John 12:1–9 presents us with an excellent one. "Martha served." There was hard work connected with that supper, and many benefited by it, but she performed it *for Him.* "They made *Him* a supper." That was true service done out of a full heart of gratitude to the One who had brought her brother from the tomb.

Lazarus "sat at the table *with Him*," a type of that communion with the Master which alone gives point and character to either service or worship.

Mary took the costly ointment and anointed the feet of Jesus. Upon Him she lavished it all. It was the outflow of a heart concentrated upon Christ, though the odour of the ointment filled the house. The worship of the heart is fragrant everywhere.

The Father is seeking worshippers (John 4:23). The Lord has need of servants (2 Tim. 2:1–7). May we respond to both desires!

In speaking of worship, do you intend to refer to your form of worship as compared with that of other people?

Not at all. I have no form of worship, whatever other people may have. To the Jews of old God gave what might be termed a "form of worship." But it was of a national, outward, ceremonial sort, though acceptable to God, if carried out with all the heart. Alas! it was not so, and soon Jehovah had to say: "In vain do they worship Me."

But the shadow dispensation has passed away and the substance has come. Christian worship is not national, not a mere matter of the lips, not a thing made up of certain ceremonies and observances. You can no more confine worship in forms than you can keep new wine in old bottles. The thing has been attempted times without number, for again and again have even true believers drifted back in mind and understanding to pre-Christian days. The result, however, must either be that if true worship be retained the forms are burst and discarded, or that if the forms be rigidly adhered to the new wine of true worship is spilled and quickly disappears.

You speak of worship and service. Is there such a very great difference between them? Ought we not to worship God whenever we go to a service?

There is a very distinct difference. But just as we are speaking of worship and not "a form of worship," so we are speaking of service, and not "a service." The fact is, in the minds of many the whole subject is obscurred and confused to a surprising degree, until no clear scriptural idea is left.

We have heard of a preacher who rose from his seat one Sunday morning and said: "Let us commence the *worship of* Almighty God by singing the hymn—

"Come ye sinners poor and needy,
Weak and wounded, sick and sore."

To him "worship" evidently meant any kind of religious meeting. But it does not! It may be a true service to the Lord on the part of the preacher to conduct a meeting for the edification of believers or the conversion of sinners. It is no service (in the proper sense of the word) for the listeners. And for neither preacher nor hearers is it worship. Worship is not hearing sermons nor preaching them. Nor is it praying, or singing Gospel hymns. It is that up-flow of adoration which rises from a redeemed soul to God.

Are worship and service confined to any particular class, or may all Christians have part in them?

All Christians are both priests and servants. We read for instance:
"Ye also ... are built up ... an holy priesthood, to offer up spiritual sacrifices, acceptable to God by Jesus Christ" (1 Peter 2:5).
And again:
"Ye are ... a royal priesthood ... that ye should show forth the praises of Him who hath called you out of darkness into His marvellous light" (1 Peter 2:9).
These words were written not to clergy, but to Christians. All such are a holy and a royal priesthood. Mark their activities! In the one character they OFFER UP spiritual sacrifices to God, *i.e.*, worship. In the other they SHOW FORTH the praises of God, *i.e.*, service.

In connection with service it is, of course, true that not every Christian has a gift according to 1 Corinthians 12, nor is an evangelist, pastor, or teacher according to Ephesians 4. Yet every Christian can serve according to Romans 12. If he cannot prophesy or teach, he can show hospitality, or mercy; he can bless his persecutors, or weep in sympathy with a weeping saint, and thus be "serving the Lord."

Are there any special qualifications needed for us
to worship or serve God rightly?

As to worship, Hebrews 10:19–22 speaks of "boldness to enter
into the holiest by the blood of Jesus," and we are exhorted to draw near
with "a true heart in full assurance of faith." These are two important
qualifications. Faith must be in active exercise, so that there is full assurance based upon the work of Christ, not a doubt or fear left. Then a true
heart would indicate that sincerity and transparency of soul which is the
result of a tender conscience and self-judgment.

As to service, read Acts 20:17–35. Here is one of the most eminent
of Christ's servant's reviewing his career. Our service may be of the most
insignificant description, yet the things that marked him should characterize us. Here are some of them: "humility of mind;" "many tears" —
expressive of much exercise; "none of these things move me" — stability
of soul; "I have coveted no man's silver, or gold, or apparel" — the
strictest possible righteousness before the world; "I have shewed you all
things" — the practice of what is preached. These are important qualifications indeed.

If a person recently converted desires to serve the
Lord, how would you advise them to start?

I would encourage all young believers to serve the Lord by just
doing that thing which, in His ordering of their lives, is next to hand.
"Do the next thing," is a very sound motto, albeit that, as a rule, it is the
very thing we do *not* wish to do.

Years ago there was living in a mountainous district of Virginia a
humble servant-girl, who had never had more than three months' school-
ing in her life. She earned four dollars a month. Out of this, one dollar
went to her chapel, and one dollar to foreign missions. She was the
largest local contributor in both these directions. The other two dollars
went to her father, who was very poor and had a large family. She clothed
herself by taking in sewing and sitting up late to do it.

An earnest minister visited the place. Accommodation was scarce,
so her room was handed over to him. On the table lay her Bible. He

opened it and found it marked on nearly every page. But what struck him most of all was her note against "Go ye into all the world" (Mark 16:15). In firm, clear letters it stood, "Oh, if I could!"

Next day he spoke to her about it, whereupon she broke into crying, and for the moment he could get nothing out of her. Later on he heard this story.

She was converted at the age of fourteen, and on reaching home found a paper, "China's Call for the Gospel," lying about. Where it came from nobody knew. That had coloured all her thoughts. For ten years she had prayed the Lord to send her to China.

But lately a change had come over her. Just two weeks before, she had come to the conclusion that she had made a mistake, and that, after all, the Lord's plan for her was that she should be a missionary in the kitchen. At once her prayer became, "Make me willing to be a missionary for Thee in the kitchen," and the Lord had answered that prayer.

For ten years she had longed for the big thing, while not neglecting smaller things, as her contributions showed. At last she became willing to accept the *very little* thing, to shine for the Lord in that narrow circle as kitchen-maid, *and then the Lord despatched her to some very blessed service in China*! For the minister became convinced that he was specially sent there of God to help her, and to China she ultimately went.

May service of that kind be greatly multiplied on every hand!

"He that is faithful in that which is least is faithful also in much" (Luke 16:10).

Chapter Twenty-two

THE RAPTURE
AND
THE APPEARING

It is an actual fact that the Lord Jesus Christ is coming back again! Yet many people, even true believers, seem hardly to believe it. It seems to them a dreamy, visionary, mystical idea, and they cannot help thinking that the enthusiasts who announce it must be mistaking figures of speech for sober facts.

But, after all, why should you be surprised? You believe that He has been here once. Then why not twice?

Consider for a moment what happened when He first came. He was rejected, and His life was cut short. His public mission of three and a half years closed in His sudden death. But being God manifest in flesh, in dying He wrought redemption for His people; He rose again. Is it likely that the story ends there as far as this earth is concerned? Shall the ejection of the Creator from the world by the creature be the last word? By no means. Men despised Him in His humiliation. He will surely return in His glory.

We are not left, however, to consider what seems likely or reasonable. The doctrine of the Second Advent is one of the commonest themes of Scripture. The Old Testament frequently refers to it. In the New Testament the full truth of it is plainly revealed. From the great mass of texts that might be quoted, let us select one which is singularly explicit.

"Ye men of Galilee, why stand ye gazing up into heaven? this same Jesus, which is taken up from you into heaven, shall so come in like manner as ye have seen Him go into heaven" (Acts 1:11).

This message has about it almost the sound of a legal document. Lawyers write a very simple statement in a rather lengthy way because they find it needful to hedge about their words from possible mis-interpretations. So here there is a fulness and almost a redundancy of expression, especially designed to foil any attempt to evade or mystify this great fact.

It is evident from this verse that the Lord Jesus is Himself coming just as He went. How did He go? Personally; then personally He will come. He went actually as a living Man — it was no spirit mani-festation. Then actually as a living Man He will come. He went visibly; visibly He will come. He went from the earth. Then to the earth He will return.

The attentive Christian reader, however, is often puzzled as he pursues his studies into this great truth, by seeming discrepancies between different passages, and he needs to have placed in his hands the key that unlocks the door of difficulty.

That key is an understanding of the difference between the two stages of the Second Advent, which for the sake of brevity we term "The Rapture" (*i.e.*, "the catching-up") and "The Appearing."

Take the trouble at this point to thoughtfully read 1 Thessalonians 4:13 to 5:3. Notice that the Thessalonian believers were troubled because some of their number had died, and they thought that they would there-fore miss the glory of the appearing and reign of Christ. Paul tells them not to sorrow, because as certainly as Jesus died and rose again, God will bring WITH Jesus all such when He comes (verse 14). Then the Apostle explains how this is to be brought about, by what means the formerly dead in Christ are found with Him in bodies of glory so as to be able to share in His glorious appearing.

This explanation is prefaced by "this we say unto you by the word of the Lord," indicating that what follows is not something which had been previously made known, but something newly revealed: his author-ity for stating it being not Old Testament scripture, nor any previous utterance, but the direct revelation of the Lord.

And this is the explanation: "The Lord Himself shall descend from heaven with a shout ... and the dead in Christ shall rise first: then we which are alive and remain shall be caught up together with them in the clouds, to meet the Lord in the air: and so shall we ever be with the Lord."

Now compare these words with what is written in 1 Corinthians 15:51–54, and you will find an additional fact stated. "The dead shall be raised incorruptible, and we shall be changed."

In the light of these two scriptures we gather that

(1) The Lord Himself shall descend into the air with an assembling shout.

(2) His shout will awaken the sleeping saints and raise them in bodies of glory.

(3) We, the living, will then undergo a corresponding change into a glorified condition.

(4) All believers, whether previously dead or living, will be caught up together, to be for ever with the Lord.

Oh, most blessed hour, the fruition of our long-cherished hope!

All this, however, leaves the great world untouched, save as the sudden disappearance of multitudes of saints may affect it. But the hour of retribution follows on. Hence 1 Thessalonians 5 opens by drawing a distinction between the coming of the Lord for His saints with which chapter 4 has dealt, and "the day of the Lord." That comes, not as a bridegroom for his bride, but "as a thief in the night."

When the Lord Jesus in humiliation was led as a lamb to the slaughter, He said to His enemies, "This is your hour, and the power of darkness" (Luke 22:53). But the tables are to be completely turned. He comes not in humiliation, but in glory; not as a lamb to the slaughter, but as the Lion of the tribe of Judah; not solitary and alone, but "with ten thousands of His saints"; not submitting to the will of His enemies, but that His enemies may be made His footstool. It is not man's little hour, and the short-lived triumph of evil; it is the great and dreadful day of the Lord.

"The day of the Lord" is not a day of twenty-four hours, but an interval of time, like "the day of salvation." It is a period in the cycle of "times and seasons" marked by the absolute supremacy and authority of the Lord. It starts with His public manifestation in the clouds of heaven — His appearing with His saints.

It is to this public appearing that Old Testament prophets so frequently refer, being the consummation of God's ways with Israel and the earth. It ushers in a short, sharp work of judgment whereby the earth is purged of its dross before the shining forth of glory in the millennial reign of Christ.

Before this public appearing certain things must take place as foretold in Scripture. The Lord Jesus Himself plainly predicted certain things (Matt. 24; Mark 13; Luke 21). Again 2 Thessalonians 2 shows us that before the day of Christ comes there must first be "a falling away," an apostasy, and connected with that, the revelation of *the man of sin*, commonly called "antichrist." In him sin will find its culminating expression. He will be its very embodiment.

When the iniquity of man rises then to its full height God will smite in judgment. The Lord Jesus, who once bore judgment for our sakes, is then to be its Executor, and that oldest of all prophecies given through the lips of a man will be fulfilled: "Behold, the Lord cometh with ten thousands of His saints to execute judgment upon all" (Jude 14, 15). Previously the saints will have been "changed" according to 1 Corinthians 15, and "caught up" according to 1 Thessalonians 4, hence they are with Him in a glorified condition, and when the heavens open and reveal Him in the "flaming fire" of judgment, they are with Him, and He will be "glorified in His saints" and "admired in all them that believe . . . in that day" (2 Thess.1:7–10).

Meanwhile our business is "to serve the living and true God, and to wait for His Son from heaven" (1 Thess. 1:9, 10).

May not what you call *the Rapture* be just a beautiful and poetic way of speaking of the death of a saint, and *the Appearing* be what is commonly called "the end of the world"?

The death of a saint is thus described in Scripture: "To depart and to be with Christ" (Phil. 1:23). Is there no difference between *our going* to be with Christ and *His coming* for us? Further, when the saint dies and goes to be with Christ, his body is laid IN the grave. When Christ comes for His saints according to 1 Thessalonians 4, He takes all their bodies OUT of the graves. Are these one and the same thing?

No. The coming of the Lord *for* His saints is not death, but the deliverance of His people from the last vestige of death. The appearing of

Christ *with* His saints is not "the end of the world," by which people generally mean the winding up of the heavens and the earth in their present condition. Revelation 19, speaks of the Lord's appearing in glory. Chapter 20 shows the result, Satan restrained and a thousand years of blessing for this weary old earth. After that — the end.

In this case would there not be two comings, a third Advent after the second?

No. Frequently in Scripture the coming of the Lord is spoken of in a general way without referring definitely to either of its two stages. The Rapture and the Appearing are only two parts or stages of the one coming. When the Queen visits the City of London in state, the Lord Mayor and sheriffs meet her at Temple Bar, and after certain ceremonies they take their place in the procession behind her and re-enter the City, accompanying her to the Guildhall or wherever she is going.

Even so will it be at the coming of Christ. Caught up into the air to meet Him, we shall shortly after return with Him to share in His glorious kingdom.

What signs should we look for as indicating that the Lord's coming is near?

If the appearing be in question, then such scriptures as 2 Thessalonians 2, 2 Timothy 3, and Matthew 24. supply the answer. The rising tide of apostasy in Christendom; the prevalence of false prophets deceiving many; the extraordinary awakening of the Jewish race, *i.e.*, the fig tree putting forth leaves according to Matthew 24:32; the increasing carelessness of the world deceived into false security by its own achievements and saying "Peace and safety"; all these things and others of which we are witnesses indicate that we draw nigh to the end of this age.

But all these things are portents of the Appearing. As to the Rapture which precedes it, no signs are to be looked for. It is an event outside the calculation of times and seasons. These belong to the earth, as the opening verse of 1 Thessalonians 5 shows, and there was no need for the apostle to write to the Thessalonians on the subject. But as to the

Rapture, which is not connected with times and seasons, there was a very distinct need that he should write to them.

There is nothing awaiting fulfilment before Christ comes *for* His saints. He may come at any moment.

Must not the world be converted first?

That question would not be asked were it not that an unscriptural idea exists on the subject. Nowhere in the Bible is the conversion of the whole world by preaching of the Gospel either stated or implied. The Gospel is preached by command of God for the gathering out of the nations a people for His Name (Acts 15:14). The world will not be converted, but rather purified by judgment which will remove the workers of evil and subjugate the earth to God. "When *Thy judgments* [not *Thy Gospel*] are in the earth, the inhabitants of the world will learn righteousness" (Isa. 26:9).

Will all Christians be caught up at the Rapture?

Undoubtedly. To illustrate the truth of the Rapture, the effect of a strong magnet held over steel filings when mixed with sand has been used. It is a good illustration, only this must be remembered: Christians are not only like so many individual steel filings, they are by the Holy Ghost livingly connected together. They are "one flock," one family, "one body." When the Lord Jesus comes He will take His Church as one living entity, His body and His bride. Mutilated fragments will not be left behind.

The idea that some Christians will be left behind seems to crop up in two directions.

First, we have the prophets of various latter-day apostasies from the truth. Some of them teach only "living," "faithful," "watching" Christians will be taken. Their "faithfulness" is manifested by their reception of the teachings of the false prophet in question! Comment on this is needless.

Secondly, true Christians have run away with the idea that only "watching" believers are caught up, from such a Scripture as the following: "Unto *them that look for Him* shall He appear the second time without sin unto salvation" (Heb. 9:28).

After all, however, where can you find a true Christian who is not looking for Him? You can find many who are very unintelligent, who do not understand the truth of His coming, who have never heard of "the Rapture." Yet they look for Christ. *He* is the hope of their hearts, though they know not how that hope shall be fulfilled.

The fact is, the expression "them that look for Him," like "them that love God," (Rom. 8:28) is just a Bible way of describing *believers*. If a man does not love God, nor look for Christ, he cannot be called a Christian.

After all, is not this teaching concerning the Second Advent rather speculative? Is there any real use in it?

It is no more speculative than the teaching divinely given to Noah concerning the approaching flood, or the prophecies given to Israel during centuries concerning the first coming of the Saviour. Difficulties may be raised as to details where Scripture is silent, and men may disagree and mystify matters as to the second coming just as the scribes succeeded in mystifying their generation as to the first coming. But the broad outlines of the truth as to it stand clear and plain in Scripture, and the event is sure.

As to the use of this truth, it will be found in practice that no fact exercises a more solemnizing effect on the consciences of sinners. No truth has a more separating effect upon believers. Shall we join hand in hand with the world which is shortly to come under judgment? No. "Every man that hath this hope in Him [Christ] purifieth himself even as He is pure" (1 John 3:3). He whose hope is in Christ and His speedy return puts far from him every defiling thing.

Do you believe that the "Rapture of the saints" is now very near?

Yes. Foolish attempts have been made to fix dates for the Lord's return, thus contravening His own words. Earnest believers, too, have allowed themselves to use extravagant language, giving the impression that they were certain it could not be distant more than a year or two. Years have passed, and those who listened to these expressions have become sceptical as to the whole thing.

The truth remains, however: He *is* coming, and that *quickly.* Everything, both in the church and in the world, points to the closing up of this age. Therefore we lift up our heads and expect Him.

Entering a Christian's room the other day my eye fell on these words framed like a text and hung on the wall,

"PERHAPS TO-DAY."

I knew what it meant. That is the right attitude. His coming is certainly near. May we rise each morning with this thought: *perhaps He may come to-day*; and may we so purify ourselves in holiness before Him that our unchecked response may gladly be: "Even so, come, Lord Jesus."